ISTEP+ Coach

English/Language Arts

LEVEL

G

Triple SSS Press Media Development

ISTEP+ Coach, English/Language Arts, Level G
06IN
ISBN# 1-58620-458-0

EVP, Publisher: Steven Zweig
Managing Editor: Steve Bedney
Creative Director: Spencer Brinker
Art Director: Farzana Razak

Developmental Editor: Justin Trewartha
Editor: Amy Christensen

Designer: Otto Sanchez
Cover Design: Farzana Razak
Production Manager: Michelle McGuinness
Contributing Author: Triple SSS Press Media Development
Cover Photo: Robert Llewellyn/Corbis

Triumph Learning 333 East 38th Street, New York, NY 10016-2777
©2004 Triumph Learning, LLC
A Haights Cross Communications company

10 9 8 7 6 5 4 3 2 1

Table of Contents

	Indiana's Academic Standards/ Indicators

Introduction

Every year, the state of Indiana gives an English/Language Arts test called the ISTEP+ in order to find out what students have learned in reading and writing.

The ISTEP+ does <u>not</u> test how many reading and writing details students have memorized. It is a test of how well they understand some of the important ideas and skills necessary to be good readers and writers.

This book, the **ISTEP+ *Coach, English/Language Arts, Level H***, was written to help students sharpen their English/Language Arts skills and prepare for the test.

The ***Coach*** consists of Units that are divided into chapters and lessons, following the structure of the Indiana Standards. These lessons will help prepare students in the following ways:

1. Every lesson focuses on teaching a single skill within a Standard known as an Indicator.

2. After instruction on the Indicator, the lesson provides Example questions. The discussion after each Example question helps students understand how to answer the question by walking them through the thinking behind the correct answer.

3. Finally, the *Selections for Practice* at the end of each Unit provide plenty of practice and assess what students have learned by asking test-like questions.

Work through the book carefully. Please remember that the concept, or "big idea," behind an answer is more important than the answer itself. There are no shortcuts to doing well on the ISTEP+ Test. Students should study hard and let the ***ISTEP+ Coach English/Language Arts, Level H*** guide them to success. Good Luck!

Unit 1 — Word Recognition, Fluency, and Vocabulary Development

The Indiana Indicators addressed in this unit include:

7.1.1 Students should be able to identify and understand idioms and comparisons—such as analogies, metaphors, and similes—in prose and poetry.

7.1.2 Students should be able to use knowledge of Greek, Latin, and Anglo-Saxon roots and word parts to understand subject-area vocabulary.

7.1.3 Students should be able to clarify word meanings through the use of definition, example, restatement, or through the use of contrast stated in the text.

GETTING the IDEA

In order to be an effective reader you must be able to understand the words and phrases that writers use. Usually, you will not have much trouble with most common reading materials, but everyone, from time to time, comes across words and phrases or expressions whose meaning he or she does not know.

This unit addresses word recognition, including how to determine the meaning of a word by considering the context in which it is used. This strategy involves considering how the word is used in the sentence, and what it would have to mean for the sentence to make sense.

The unit also discusses word recognition through the use of analogies, which help you to make connections between different words and concepts.

Finally, Chapter 1 explains the difference between a simile and a metaphor. A simile is a direct comparison that uses *like* or *as*. A metaphor is an implied comparison, rather than a direct comparison. This chapter will also help you to understand what authors are trying to say when they use these comparisons in their writing.

Vocabulary and Concept Development

Context Clues

Sometimes when you are reading, you come across a word that you do not know. When this happens, what do you do? You could get up from your desk, go find a dictionary, look the word up, and then go back to your reading, but that would be time consuming and would disrupt your train of thought. You also cannot get up from your desk to look up words during a test. However, there is another way that you can often use to determine the meaning of a word on your own.

Context refers to the other words in the sentence and the general meaning of the sentence and paragraph. By considering the context in which a word is used, you can often figure out what it means. For example, let's say that you came across the following sentence:

> I usually have an orange with breakfast, but today I decided to try a <u>kumquat</u> instead.

Even if you do not know what a kumquat is, you could still get a general idea of what it refers to by reading the rest of the sentence and considering the context in which *kumquat* is used. The first part of the sentence, "I usually have an orange with breakfast," indicates that when the writer has breakfast, he or she usually also has an orange.

That's easy enough to understand, so now look at the second part of the sentence, "but today I decided to try a kumquat instead." Even without knowing what a kumquat is, you can figure out that the writer is trying to say that he or she did not have an orange for breakfast, but instead had something called a kumquat. You can figure out what it means by using context. To do this, try reading the sentence again, replacing *kumquat* with a blank space.

> I usually have an orange with breakfast, but today I decided to try a _____ instead.

Now try to fill that space in with a word or phrase that you think would fit. The most logical replacements would be an apple, a banana, or some other food. By using context, you can determine that a kumquat is something that you can eat. You might even go so far as to say that it is another type of fruit, which it is. A kumquat is a type of citrus fruit, very similar to an orange.

Now let's try using context to determine the meaning of a verb. Consider this sentence:

> *While Margaret tried on one outfit after another in the dressing room, Phillip merely stood and <u>tarried</u>.*

What does the word *tarried* mean? Again, let's look at the context of the sentence. We know that there are two people, Margaret and Phillip. They appear to be in a clothing store because Margaret is trying on clothes. Philip is merely standing and tarrying. What words or phrases could you replace *tarried* with? Since he is just standing there, we know he's not running or dancing, nor does he seem to be engaged in any other type of activity, such as reading or whistling. In fact, it seems like he is just standing there and waiting, which he is. To *tarry* is to wait.

Even if you cannot determine the exact meaning of a word by using context, you can usually get a general enough idea to get by in your reading until you have a chance to look words up later.

EXAMPLE 1

She asked me to place our order in French at the fancy restaurant. Unfortunately, I could not because I only know a smattering of that language.

What is a *smattering*?

Ⓐ   a form of written communication

Ⓑ   a dialect

Ⓒ   a small amount of knowledge

Ⓓ   a great amount of knowledge

A *smattering* is a small amount of knowledge about something, in this case, the French language. By considering the context in which the word is used, you know that it does not mean "a great amount of knowledge" because the sentence uses the word *only*. The other choices, "a form of written communication" and "a dialect," do not make sense in the context of the sentence.

EXAMPLE 2

When we returned to the farm that night, there was a flock of magpies circling overhead. They had been gnawing at the cornstalks all day and had ruined much of the crop.

What is a magpie?

Ⓐ   a breed of camel

Ⓑ   a type of bird

Ⓒ   a type of helicopter

Ⓓ   a child that is misbehaving

A magpie is a type of bird. From this sentence, you know that a magpie is something that is part of a flock, flies, and eats corn, meaning that it is most likely some type of bird.

Idioms

An **idiom** is an expression that cannot be understood just by knowing the meanings of the words in the expression. Expressions such as "get your feet wet" and "drop someone a line" do not literally mean what they say, but rather refer to something else. For example, to "get your feet wet" means to get started with something, or to start to be exposed to, or become familiar with something. It is meant to refer to getting into the water at a beach or lake. The water is often cold, and getting in can be a shock to your body. The first step toward getting in, though, is to step in, or to get your feet wet. Dropping someone a line means to send a message. It means contact will be made, usually informally.

When faced with an idiom, you may not always know what it refers to, which can make understanding it a bit difficult. The best way to determine what an idiom means is to, again, consider the context in which it is being used. For example, someone might say to you,

> Don't go outside now! It's _raining cats and dogs_ out there!
> You'll get soaked!

The speaker would not literally mean that there are house pets falling from the sky. By considering the context in which the phrase "raining cats and dogs" is used, you can determine that it means that it is raining very hard, because going outside will mean that you will get very wet.

Another way to figure out what an idiom is trying to say is by figuring out what situation or condition the idiom is literally referring to. For example, what if someone said to you,

> _Keep an eye out_ for Dennis. He should be here any minute.

The literal meaning of this phrase would lead you to believe that the speaker wanted you to take your eye out of your head, which is obviously not true. The central word in this phrase is _eye_, which is something we use to see or look with. What the speaker is actually trying to say is something along the lines of "look for Dennis," but more specifically, "We know that Dennis is coming, so be aware that you should look around for him and expect to see him soon."

Idioms can be hard to figure out if you are not familiar with them. On the next page is a chart of commonly used idioms and what they mean. Read through the list and familiarize yourself with them.

Idiom	Meaning	Example
and then some	everything previously mentioned, and even more	We got everything we wanted, and then some!
at the eleventh hour	last-minute or with very little time left	She stepped in at the eleventh hour to help us out.
fed up with	to run out of patience	I'm fed up with all of this arguing!
on the go	to be very busy	I've been on the go all day.
bent out of shape	overly worried about something	He was all bent out of shape about not finishing his homework before dinner.
break a leg	to wish someone luck	Just before she went on, everyone told the actress to break a leg.
burn the midnight oil	work very late	It's due tomorrow morning, so I guess I'll be burning the midnight oil tonight.
by the skin of one's teeth	just barely	I just barely got it done on time. I finished by the skin of my teeth.
call it a day	stop working for the day	We finished all of our work early, so we decided to call it a day.
do a bang-up job	to do something very well	Sheila did a bang-up job on the test.
down in the dumps	depressed	He was down in the dumps for a week after breaking up with his girlfriend.
elbow grease	hard work	A fresh coat of paint and a little elbow grease is all we need to make that car as good as new.

Idiom	Meaning	Example
flash in the pan	a passing fad	That rock band was a flash in the pan.
get a kick out of something	to find something amusing	I got a kick out of the way the kids dressed up for Halloween.
in the black	making a profit	Sales are up. We're finally in the black!
in the red	to be in debt	Sales dropped off. We're in the red now.
keep your chin up	be optimistic; remain brave	I know things are bad now, but keep your chin up.
leave well enough alone	do not do anything, because you will only make things worse	You've interfered enough! Just leave well enough alone!
make a mountain out of a molehill	to turn a small problem into a big one	It's not a big deal. Don't make a mountain out of a molehill.
pull someone's leg	try to fool someone	She said she was sick, but I think she was just pulling my leg.
right off the bat	immediately; without delay	I should have asked him to leave right off the bat.
shoot the breeze	have a casual conversation	We just shot the breeze while we waited for the others to arrive.
two-faced	deceitful	That two-faced salesman said he'd give me a deal then he overcharged me!
under the weather	sick	He's feeling a little under the weather.

EXAMPLE 3

Karen got bent out of shape when I told her the project wouldn't be finished until tomorrow.

What did Karen do?

Ⓐ   said bad things about someone

Ⓑ   got overly worried

Ⓒ   decided to take it easy

Ⓓ   hurt herself stretching

When someone gets bent out of shape, he or she becomes overly worried about something that is not significantly important.

EXAMPLE 4

It's only going to be a day late. Don't go making a mountain out of a molehill.

What is the speaker telling the listener not to do?

Ⓐ   stay too long

Ⓑ   ruin the landscape

Ⓒ   lose confidence

Ⓓ   turn a small problem into a big problem

Your Teacher Will Discuss Your Answer

Analogies

An analogy is a comparison of the similar aspects of two different things. To identify or complete an analogy, consider the relationship between the two things that have been identified. For example:

Dog is to cat as _____ is to mouse

First you need to figure out what the relationship is between the dog and the cat. Think about the basic things you know about cats and dogs. Both are four-legged, furry house pets. Both are mammals, and dogs traditionally chase cats.

Now you need to determine how to finish the analogy. What relates to the mouse in the same way that the dog relates to the cat? A mouse is not a house pet, but it is a mammal. Unfortunately, there are literally thousands of mammals, so that is probably not the answer. Dogs chase cats—what chases mice? Cats. The complete analogy should look like this:

Dog is to cat as cat is to mouse.

Sometimes analogies will be obvious, and other times you will need to stop and think about them. Always be sure to identify the ways in which items compare before attempting to complete an analogy.

EXAMPLE 5

Boy is to man as _____ is to woman.

Ⓐ man

Ⓑ girl

Ⓒ mother

Ⓓ baby

A boy is a child that grows into a man, so the question is, who grows into a woman? While choice D, baby, makes some sense, choice B is better because it identifies a specific gender. A baby could be either a little boy or a little girl.

EXAMPLE 6

Pajamas are to nighttime as a business suit is to _____ .

Ⓐ   snack time

Ⓑ   noon time

Ⓒ   daytime

Ⓓ   a bathing suit

Pajamas are the type of clothes you wear at nighttime, and a business suit is something you would wear during the daytime.

Figurative Word Use: Similes and Metaphors

The words and phrases people use are not always meant to be taken strictly as they are said. Most of us use figurative language when we speak and write, meaning that we use words and phrases that refer to things in terms of other things. For example, say your friend told you, "That guy is a jailbird."

Your friend would not mean that the person was literally a bird that lived in jail, but rather that the person in question has spent a great deal of time in prison and/or is a habitual criminal.

Figurative language and figures of speech are used because they make communication more interesting and can add greater meaning to what we are trying to say or write. The two most common forms of figurative word use are similes and metaphors.

A **simile** is a comparison of two unlike things, using either *as* or *like* as a connecting word. When you use a simile to make a comparison, you create an image in the reader's mind that connects qualities of the two items you are comparing. For example:

> *The child was as quiet as a mouse.*

The person writing this sentence does not literally mean that the child only made high-pitched squeaks from time to time. Instead, the writer is saying that the child made very little noise, just as a mouse makes very little noise.

The comparison drawn in a simile often involves some degree of exaggeration. For example,

> *John was as cold as ice.*

In this sentence, John is compared to the temperature of ice. In other words, John is indifferent. However, John is not *actually* the temperature of ice. This is merely an exaggeration to make a point.

EXAMPLE 7

Which of the following is a simile?

Ⓐ   Larry liked the way his mother cooked.

Ⓑ   As I was saying, we should not throw rocks at each other.

Ⓒ   She sings like an angel.

Ⓓ   His was blue, and mine was green.

The two things being compared are the singing of the girl and the singing of an angel, with *like* as the connecting word. It is not enough for a sentence to contain the words *like* or *as*—there must also be a comparison.

EXAMPLE 8

Which simile would you use if you wanted to indicate that something was slow?

Ⓐ   like a kangaroo

Ⓑ   as a cat

Ⓒ   like a flash

Ⓓ   as a snail

The phrase "as a snail" refers to the slowness of a snail's crawl. You might use choice A if you wanted to say "he was jumpy like a kangaroo" or choice B if you wanted to say "she was as sleek as a cat." You might use choice C if you wanted to say "he was quick like a flash."

EXAMPLE 9

Which of the following words is generally used with a simile?

(A)   as

(B)   an

(C)   and

(D)   are

Similes require the use of the word *like* or the word *as*. The other three choices may or may not be included when using similes.

EXAMPLE 10

Sherman can run very fast.

Choose the BEST way to rewrite this sentence, using a simile.

(A)   Sherman runs as fast as molasses.

(B)   Sherman can run like the wind.

(C)   Sherman likes to run.

(D)   Sherman is not a slowpoke.

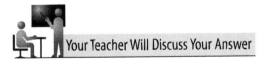 Your Teacher Will Discuss Your Answer

A **metaphor** is also a form of comparison of two unlike things, but it does not use *like* or *as*. Instead, a metaphor is a figure of speech in which one thing is described in terms of another, often (but not always) using a version of the verb "to be." A metaphor is an implied comparison. It establishes an immediate relationship between the two items being compared, sometimes leaving the specific aspect of the comparison up to the reader to determine. For example,

> *Todd is a stick in the mud.*

In this sentence, the writer implies that Todd is a piece of wood in mud. The person writing this means that Todd is old-fashioned or boring and doesn't like to join in with others. Again, there is a certain degree of exaggeration involved, as it is unlikely that Todd never joins in with others. By using the metaphor, the writer immediately creates in the reader's mind an image of Todd as a person who is not a great deal of fun.

EXAMPLE 11

Which of the following is a metaphor?

Ⓐ   Darlene is as skinny as a pole.

Ⓑ   Jeannie can dance as beautifully as a ballerina.

Ⓒ   Donny drives like a professional racer.

Ⓓ   Raoul is a weasel.

In this sentence, the writer may be comparing the sneakiness of Raoul with the sneakiness of a weasel, without specifically stating so. Sometimes the word *weasel* is also used to describe someone who is sneaky or cannot be trusted. It is left up to the reader to determine which aspects of Raoul are being compared to a weasel.

EXAMPLE 12

Elaine is smart.

Choose the BEST way to rewrite this sentence, using a metaphor.

Ⓐ   Elaine is as smart as a whip.

Ⓑ   Elaine is an ox.

Ⓒ   Elaine is really, really smart.

Ⓓ   Elaine is a walking encyclopedia.

While Elaine is not really a walking encyclopedia, the writer is implying that Elaine has a vast knowledge of information, suggesting that she is smart. Choice A is incorrect because it is a simile, not a metaphor. Choice B is a metaphor, but it implies that Elaine is dull, not smart. Choice C is incorrect because it does not draw any form of comparison—it simply restates that Elaine is smart.

EXAMPLE 13

Which metaphor would you use when describing stars?

Ⓐ   There were millions of twinkling lanterns in the night sky.

Ⓑ   A dark cloud descended upon the town.

Ⓒ   Money is the root of all evil.

Ⓓ   Life is a bowl of cherries.

The metaphor in choice A implies that the stars in the sky resembled tiny, twinkling lights. The sentence does not literally mean that there were lanterns hanging in the sky. Choice B might be used to indicate that bad luck had befallen a town, and choice C indicates that greed drives people to do bad things. Choice D is a metaphor that essentially says that life is good.

EXAMPLE 14

When would you want to use a metaphor?

Ⓐ   when you want to make a direct comparison

Ⓑ   when you want to make an implied comparison

Ⓒ   when you want to specifically describe physical qualities

Ⓓ   when making a scientific report

Metaphors are used to make an indirect or implied comparison. A simile is a direct comparison, using the words *like* or *as*.

Common Roots and Word Parts

A **root** is a word or a part of a word to which a **prefix** (something added to the beginning of a word) or **suffix** (something added to the end of a word) could be added to make a new word. Many roots and word parts come from Greek, Latin, and Anglo-Saxon languages, which influenced the evolution of the English language, and whose words are reflected in our usage today.

Common roots and word parts include these:

Root	Refers to	Example
aero	air	aerodynamic—moves easily through the air
agri	land/dirt	agribusiness—business related to farming
angio	blood vessels	angioma—a tumor made of heart vessels
ante	before	anterior—situated at the front of something
arch	ancient	archeology—study of ancient civilizations
astra	stars	astronomy—the study of stars
audi/aur	hearing/ear	audible—capable of being heard
auto	self	autonomy—control over oneself
be	thoroughly	bedazzled—completely dazzled
bene	good	beneficial—for the goodness of something
bio	life	biology—the study of life
cardio	the heart	cardiac—of the heart
ceed/cede	to go	succeed—to go far
centi	hundredth	centimeter—a hundredth of a meter
chrono	time	chronology—timeline
circum	around	circumnavigate—to go around
com	with	comply—to go along with
cycl	circular	cyclical—going in a cycle
dec	ten	decimal—something measured in tenths
demo	people	democracy—government of the people
dent	teeth	dentist—teeth specialist
derm	skin	dermatologist—skin doctor
dict	speaking	diction—speech
dors	back	dorsad—toward the back
duc	pulling	induce—to cause something to happen
escent	becoming	luminescent—becoming luminous
ex	out of	expand—to grow
extra	beyond	extraordinary—beyond the ordinary
fix	fasten	affix—to fasten something to something else
gene	origin/birth	genetic—inherited at birth
geo	earth	geography—maps
giga	million	gigabyte—a million bytes

Root	Refers to	Example
hecto	hundred	hectogram—a hundred grams
herb	plants	herbal—made of plants
hetero	different	heterogeneous—consisting of different parts
homo	same	homogenous—made up of one thing
hydro	water	hydrate—to add water to something
inter	between	interview—discussion between two people
intra	within	introspect—looking at oneself (mentally)
jur	the law	jury—a group that makes legal decisions
kilo	thousand	kilogram—a thousand grams
logue	word or thought	dialogue—conversation
logy	study of something	biology—study of life
mal	bad	malcontent—a bad person in a group
mega	million	megabyte—a thousand bytes
meta	change	metamorphosis—to undergo a change
meter	measurement	speedometer—tool that measures speed
micro	millionth	micrometer—a millionth of a meter
milli	thousandth	millimeter—a thousandth of a meter
nano	billionth	nanosecond—a billionth of a second
neo	new	neophyte—a new convert
ocu	eye	ocular—referring to vision
path	feeling	empathy—feeling for someone
ped	child	pediatrician—children's doctor
phon	hearing	phonograph—a type of audio recording
retro	backward	retrospect—to look back
scient	knowing	scientist—one who knows
scrib	write	scribble—to write nonsense
spec	sight	spectacles—eyeglasses
tele	distant	telescope—tool used to see far away
theo	god	theology—study of God
tract	drawing to	attract—to draw to something
vert	turning	convert—turn someone to a way of thinking
vita	life	vitamin—supplement that aids health
vore	eating	voracious—having a great appetite

Those examples were only a few of the many roots and word parts that exist in the English language. Knowledge of roots and word parts can help you to analyze the meaning of complex words, such as those you'll find in science, social studies, and math. For example, consider the word *angiocardiograph*. What roots and word parts are found in this word?

- angio
- cardio
- graph

Now consider the meaning of each of these components.

Angio refers to the blood vessels.
Cardio refers to the heart.
Graph refers to writing.

When you put the three together, you come up with "writing about the heart and blood vessels," which is essentially what an angiocardiograph is—an image of a person's heart and blood vessel system.

EXAMPLE 15

Using your root and word part skills, determine which of the words below refers to the study of water.

Ⓐ   cardiology

Ⓑ   hydrology

Ⓒ   hectagram

Ⓓ   hydropathic

Hydro refers to water, and logy refers to the study of something. Therefore, *hydrology* is the study of water.

EXAMPLE 16

If you had a dorsal mark on your body, where would it be?

Ⓐ   face

Ⓑ   leg

Ⓒ   stomach

Ⓓ   back

The word *dorsal* comes from <u>dors</u>, meaning "back." The part of a shark that sticks out of the water when it swims is called a dorsal fin.

EXAMPLE 17

What does a herbivore probably do?

Ⓐ   plants flowers

Ⓑ   measures things

Ⓒ   never gets hungry

Ⓓ   eats plants

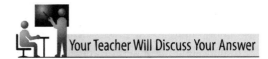 Your Teacher Will Discuss Your Answer

Unit 1

Selections for Practice

Selection 1

How Indian Summer Came to Be
adapted from the traditional Abenaki Native American tale

Long, long ago, there was a good man named Notkikad who worked hard to provide for his family. He cultivated his gardens every year to be sure that there would be plenty of food, and he always gave thanks each harvest to Tabaldak, the Master of Life.

Then one year, there was a late frost, and his crops died from the cold. Undeterred, he planted again, but then there was a drought, and his crops died of thirst. He planted a third time, but it was so late in the season that the autumn cold killed his plants.

Notkikad was very troubled. Although his wife and children had gathered some foods from the forest, it would not be enough to see them through the winter. One autumn night, he made a small fire and offered tobacco to Tabaldak and asked him for help so that he could see his family through the coming cold time. Then he went to sleep, and he dreamed. In his dream, Tabaldak came to him, telling him, "I give you these special seeds, and a time in which to plant them, Notkikad."

When he awoke, Notkikad found the seeds beside him, and although the autumn leaves were still falling from the trees, the weather was no longer cold. It seemed as if summer had returned. Notkikad and his family planted the seeds and waited for them to grow.

Within only a few days, the seeds grew rapidly, until they were ready to be harvested. Notkikad collected the crop and dried the corn, beans, and squash for the winter, and he stored the food in the wigwam. The next day, the cold winds returned, and the special season was gone.

Although we do not have Notkikad's magical seeds, we are still granted the special season each year, when the cold winds of autumn temporarily give way to the warmth of what we now call Indian Summer. It is not only a time of respite from the cold, but also a time to remember to be thankful.

Go On

Word Recognition, Fluency, and Vocabulary Development

1a. Read this sentence from the passage.

> He cultivated his gardens every year to be sure that there would be plenty of food, and he always gave thanks each harvest to Tabaldak, the Master of Life.

What does the word *cultivated* mean?

Ⓐ   destroyed

Ⓑ   moved around

Ⓒ   encouraged the growth of crops

Ⓓ   changed the contents of

1b. Read these sentences from the passage.

> Then one year, there was a late frost, and his crops died from the cold. Undeterred, he planted again, but then there was a drought, and his crops died of thirst. He planted a third time, but it was so late in the season that the autumn cold killed his plants.

What does the word *undeterred* mean?

Ⓐ   not discouraged

Ⓑ   unable to harvest crops

Ⓒ   very, very cold

Ⓓ   lacking water

Go On

1c. Read this sentence from the passage.

Notkikad collected the crop and dried the corn, beans, and squash for the winter, and he stored the food in the wigwam.

What is a "wigwam"?

Ⓐ a body of water

Ⓑ a kind of automobile

Ⓒ a section of a forest

Ⓓ a type of dwelling

1d. Which of the following sentences applies to this story?

Ⓐ Notkikad made an offering to Tabaldak and then left well enough alone.

Ⓑ Tabaldak was pulling Notkikad's leg when he gave him the seeds.

Ⓒ Notkikad was saved by Tabaldak at the eleventh hour.

Ⓓ Growing crops was a piece of cake for Notkikad.

1e. Cold wind is to autumn as _____ is to summer.

Ⓐ changing leaves

Ⓑ snow

Ⓒ rain

Ⓓ warm sunshine

Go On

Selection 2

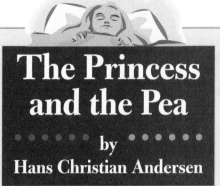

The Princess and the Pea
by
Hans Christian Andersen

Once upon a time, there was a prince that wanted to marry a real princess. To this end, he circumnavigated the globe, seeking out a true princess, but to no avail. No matter how many times he encountered women claiming to be princesses, he was never completely sure that they were. There was always something that did not seem quite right about them. Finally, he gave up and went back home, sadly. He had wished so much that he would find a real princess.

Soon after he returned, there was a terrible storm one night in the kingdom. Lightning flashes lit up the sky like daylight. The thunder boomed so deeply that it rattled the castle, and the rain came down in buckets. Then a quiet tapping was heard at the town gate. The prince's father, the old king, went out to open it and was surprised to see a young woman, drenched to the bone!

The poor young woman looked a mess. Her hair was flattened and dripping with water. Her clothes, heavy with rain, hung from her body like a scarecrow's. Her skin looked pale from the cold, and she was shivering horribly. Yet, despite her appearance, she claimed to be a princess!

The king brought her inside, and he explained the situation to his wife, the queen. "We shall see if she is really a princess," the queen thought to herself, doubtful of the girl's claim. She went to the guestroom and removed the bedding from the bed. She placed a single pea in the center of the bedstead, and then proceeded to put twenty mattresses atop the pea. Next, she put twenty eider-down beds atop the mattresses, then announced that the girl's room was ready for the night.

The next morning, she asked the young lady how she slept, and she responded, "Miserably! I could barely sleep a wink last night. There was something terribly hard in the bed, but I couldn't figure out what it was. I fear I'm black and blue all over!"

The queen instantly knew that the girl was indeed a real princess, because only a real princess could be so delicate. Soon after, the prince took her as his wife, and the two lived happily ever after.

2a. Which of the following sentences from this story contains a simile?

Ⓐ I could barely sleep a wink last night.

Ⓑ Her clothes, heavy with rain, hung from her body like a scarecrow's.

Ⓒ He had wished so much that he would find a real princess.

Ⓓ The poor young woman looked a mess.

Go On

2b. Which of the following sentences from this story contains a metaphor?

    (A)   Her hair was flattened and dripping with water.

    (B)   She placed a single pea in the center of the bedstead.

    (C)   The rain came down in buckets.

    (D)   Once upon a time, there was a prince that wanted to marry a real princess.

2c. A prince is to a king as a _____ is to a queen.

    (A)   prince

    (B)   princess

    (C)   king

    (D)   pea

2d. Read this sentence from the passage.

> To this end, he circumnavigated the globe, seeking out a true princess, but to no avail.

What does *circumnavigate* mean?

    (A)   to travel around

    (B)   to bypass

    (C)   to search

    (D)   to marry

STOP

Unit 2 Reading Comprehension

The Indiana Indicators addressed in this unit include:

7.2.1 Students should understand and analyze the differences in structure and purpose between various categories of informational materials.

7.2.2 Students should be able to locate information by using a variety of consumer and public documents.

7.2.3 Students should be able to analyze text that uses the cause-and-effect organizational pattern.

7.2.4 Students should understand how to identify and trace the development of an author's argument, point of view, or perspective in text.

7.2.5 Students should understand and explain the use of a simple mechanical device by following directions in a technical manual.

7.2.6 Students should be able to assess the adequacy, accuracy, and appropriateness of the author's evidence to support claims and assertions, noting instances of bias and stereotyping.

GETTING the IDEA

Reading comprehension refers to understanding the meaning of what you have read. Reading analysis involves thinking about what you have read and developing an opinion about some aspect of it. Unit 2 is broken down into two chapters: Chapter 2, which covers informational and technical materials, and Chapter 3, which reviews comprehension and analysis of text.

In Chapter 2, you will learn to identify different types of informational texts, such as textbooks, newspapers, and instructional or technical materials, based on their content and structure. You will also review strategies for locating information within a passage or text, and learn how to present information both in a cause-and-effect format as well as a sequential, or chronological, manner.

Chapter 3 focuses on comprehending and analyzing text, or understanding what the author is trying to say. It will help you identify the main idea of a passage and identify details that support the main idea. It will also explain what is involved in drawing inferences and making conclusions about what you are reading, and how to follow technical instructions.

Finally, you will learn how to tell the difference between a fact, something that can be independently verified, and an opinion, a belief that may or may not be held by a particular person. Your knowledge of fact and opinion will help you review methods for recognizing bias and stereotypes in writing.

Chapter 2 Informational and Technical Materials

Identifying Informational Texts

An informational text is a book, article, or encyclopedia entry written with the purpose of educating the reader about something. Different types of informational texts have different specific purposes, come in different formats, and are published at different time intervals. Some of the most common types of informational texts include:

- textbooks
- periodicals
- reference books
- instructional manuals

Textbooks

A **textbook** is a type of book written about one specific subject (such as science, English, or mathematics), and designed to be used in the classroom by a student. Textbooks may be hardcover or paperback and are generally published every few years, or as relevant material needs to be updated. Generally speaking, the books handed out to students in the classroom at the beginning of the semester are textbooks.

Periodicals

Periodicals are publications that are published at regular time intervals, such as daily, weekly, or quarterly. Newspapers and magazines are the most common forms of periodicals. They may be general-interest news publications, or specific-interest publications that focus on a single subject or profession. They are generally published on inexpensive paper, as they are not intended to be saved and reread.

Reference Books

Reference books include encyclopedias, dictionaries, and thesauruses, as well as any other type of publication designed to provide information or guidelines about specific subjects or professions. These are generally updated on a regular basis, such as annually or biennially, although the information in earlier publications usually still applies.

Manuals

A **manual** is a set of instructions about a specific machine or task. It generally contains explanations of the different parts of the machine or aspects of the task, identifies common problems and provides possible solutions, and includes contact information that the reader can use if he or she has some form of difficulty not addressed in the publication. Manuals are generally only published when a new product or process is made available to the public.

EXAMPLE 1

Which of the following would be MOST useful when studying for an exam?

Ⓐ   manual

Ⓑ   newspaper

Ⓒ   encyclopedia

Ⓓ   textbook

The textbook for a class will contain the information about which you would be tested. While you might be able to locate similar information in other types of publications, none will have it organized in the way that is best suited for studying.

EXAMPLE 2

Last week, the president announced a major policy change that would affect the structure of government. Your social studies teacher wants you to write an essay about it. Which resource should you use?

Ⓐ   textbook

Ⓑ   dictionary

Ⓒ   newspaper

Ⓓ   thesaurus

 Your Teacher Will Discuss Your Answer

Locating Information

Often when people read, they remember the basic elements of a story or written piece but not all of the specific details. When you need to recall those specific details, though, you must return to the written piece to locate the information.

In a short passage, locating information is usually not very hard because it does not take long to skim through the passage to find what you are looking for. When referring to a longer text or various types of consumer or public documents, you need to use information-location strategies such as these:

- **Look for headings and subheadings** to help you narrow your search to a specific page or section.
- **Refer to chapter names** to narrow your search to a specific chapter.
- **Refer to the table of contents or index** to locate the specific page or pages where the information can be found.

When searching for information within a chapter or passage,

- **Try remembering where you first saw the information.**
- **Read the first sentence of each paragraph** to determine whether that paragraph discusses the type of information you are looking for.
- **Skim through the passage** looking for key words or phrases related to the information you are looking for.

Finally, if you are reading a text or passage and you know that you will need to refer back to a specific piece of information, highlight or underline the information (ONLY if working with a photocopy—never highlight a textbook, library book, or any other book that does not belong to you), or make some other form of notation in the margin to help you find it again quickly when the need arises.

EXAMPLE 3

Read this passage, and then answer the question that follows.

Many people believe that the Civil War was caused by slavery and that the United States fought in World War II simply because the Japanese bombed Pearl Harbor. Actually, historical events, much like events today, generally have multiple causes.

For example, slavery was an important issue involved in the start of the Civil War, but the war was not fought so that the North could free the slaves in the South. In fact, President Lincoln himself wrote that his efforts in the war were merely to preserve the Union, whether or not it meant that slaves would be freed. One of the main causes of the war was the question of state's rights, including (but not limited to) whether a state had the right to determine for itself whether to allow slavery, or if the federal government had the authority to make the decision.

Another cause, although indirect, was the invention of the cotton gin. Prior to the invention of this machine, which partially automated the cotton producing process, slavery was growing expensive because the money plantation owners were making on selling cotton was not much more than the cost of having the slaves. If the cotton gin had not been invented, slavery likely would have ended on its own. However, this invention made cotton processing much faster and easier, meaning more cotton could be grown and sold, meaning the plantation owners could keep the slaves.

A third cause was that the manufacturing economy in the North was attracting immigrants from Europe to work in the factories, resulting in a population explosion in northern states, while populations were remaining relatively steady in the southern states. This meant that the North was getting greater representation in Congress than the South. Southerners felt this imbalance of power was unfair, because legislation benefiting northern states could be easily pushed through, whereas legislation benefiting southern states was much harder to pass.

As you can see, there were numerous factors that led to the start of the Civil War, some related to slavery, and others not. Most other major historical events also had, and continue to have, multiple causes as well.

Using your information-locating skills, identify which of the following was a cause of the Civil War.

Ⓐ   imbalance of power due to the larger population in the North

Ⓑ   the 13th Amendment, which ended slavery

Ⓒ   the bombing of Pearl Harbor

Ⓓ   the signing of the Declaration of Independence

According to the fourth paragraph, the imbalance of power in favor of the North was a cause of the Civil War. You could have found this information by skimming through the passage looking for "imbalance of power" or by looking at the first sentence in each paragraph to locate the relevant paragraph and therein find the answer.

Understanding Text Organization

The way text is organized affects the way the reader understands what he reads. It is not enough merely to have all of the necessary information; it must also be organized in a way that is logical and meaningful to those who will read it. For example, read this passage.

> *That's all there is to it! Next, turn the key all the way, until you hear the engine start. To start a car, you first need to get inside and sit in the driver's seat. As soon as the engine starts, let the key move back slightly and remove your hand. Then you need to take the key and insert it into the ignition.*

Did you understand what the writer was trying to say? Probably not. Even though this passage contains all of the important information needed about how to start a car, the way it is presented only confuses the reader. Properly ordered, though, the passage makes much more sense.

> *To start a car, you first need to get inside and sit in the driver's seat. Then you need to take the key and insert it into the ignition. Next, turn the key all the way, until you hear the engine start. As soon as the engine starts, let the key move back slightly and remove your hand. That's all there is to it!*

Most publications organize text in one of two ways:

- cause and effect
- sequence of events/chronological order

Cause and Effect

The **cause-and-effect** method organizes the information in a passage in such a way that you first identify and explain events and situations, and then you go on to write about what happened because of them. In short, first you write about the cause of something, and then you write about the effect of the cause. This method of writing is often used to explain a process, to identify the reasons why an event occurred, and to clarify the potential or actual results of certain situations or actions. For example, consider the following circumstances:

1. You stayed up late last night studying for a big test.
2. You got up early to study some more before going to school.
3. You ate a big breakfast that made you feel really full.
4. When you got to school to take the test, it was very warm in the room.
5. You fell asleep while taking the test.

The first four points are the causes and the fifth point is the effect. Because you stayed up too late and got up too early, you were tired. Eating so much and sitting in a warm room made your body want to rest. Together, these factors caused you to fall asleep. When writing a passage about this, then, you would want to talk about the first four factors, and then the fifth, because the first four caused the fifth. Your passage should look something like this:

I had a big science exam to take on Wednesday morning, so I stayed up half the night studying. Just to be sure that I really knew the material, I also woke up early to look through my notes some more. Before leaving for school, I decided to have a really big breakfast, with pancakes, syrup, some bacon and sausage, and a muffin. Boy, did I feel full when I was done!

When I got to school, I went to the room where they were giving the exam. It was pretty warm in there. When I sat down, I started to feel a bit tired. The teacher passed out the exam and I put my name on my paper. The next thing I knew, I heard the teacher announcing to the class that it was time to hand in the exam. Without even realizing it, I had fallen asleep right there at my desk!

Also, whenever something is written in a hypothetical style (what if X happened? or what if you were X?), the cause-and-effect method is generally used. For example,

If everybody wants to go together, then we'll rent a limo instead of trying to cram everybody into one car.

In this sentence, the hypothetical "If everybody wants to go together" leads directly to the effect, "we'll rent a limo instead of trying to cram everybody into one car." "If-then" statements typically involve cause and effect.

EXAMPLE 4

Read this passage, and then answer the question that follows.

All year long, Doreen had been looking forward to going to the circus. She loved to watch the trapeze artists go soaring through the air and the brave lion tamer showing off the trained animals. She always laughed whenever the clowns came out, and a shiver would run up her spine whenever the ringmaster made an announcement in his deep, booming voice.

The night before the circus, while she was supposed to be sleeping, Doreen heard her parents talking in the kitchen. "Isn't there anything we can do?" she heard her mother ask.

"No," her father replied. "Doreen has her heart set on going to the circus. We'll just have to hope that the bank will be lenient and give us another week to come up with the mortgage payment."

"But they said that if we don't pay on time this time, they're going to foreclose!"

"I know, but if we take her to the circus, we'll fall just short of being able to pay. We just can't disappoint her, though. You know how much she's been looking forward to this."

The next morning, when Doreen came downstairs, she said to her father, "Daddy, I don't think I want to go to the circus this year."

"Why not?" he asked.

"I think I'm getting a little too old for that kind of kid stuff, don't you? Why don't we all stay home and just watch television tonight. I think that would be really fun!"

Why did Doreen change her mind?

Ⓐ   She felt she was really too old to go to the circus.

Ⓑ   She didn't like the circus.

Ⓒ   Her parents told her that she couldn't go.

Ⓓ   She realized her family couldn't afford to go.

After hearing her parents' conversation, Doreen realized that money was too tight, and that if they went, it would make life very difficult for her mother and father. Although she said she didn't want to go, she really did enjoy the circus but felt that it was more important for her parents to be happy than for her to enjoy a night out.

Sequence of Events

One of the most common ways writers organize their writing is in chronological order. This means that they write events in the order in which they happened. If you were writing about how to make a sandwich, for example, you would first talk about getting a piece of bread, then about putting something on it, and finally, putting another piece of bread on top of that. This writing style helps the reader to understand what is going on, and why. For example,

> *At first, he ran right over to me when I called. It was Sunday afternoon, meaning it was time to give Rover, our dog, his weekly bath. I had to chase him around the house several times before I caught him. I first went into the bathroom and filled the tub with water because I knew he wouldn't sit and wait quietly for me to fill it after I brought him into the bathroom. When he realized that I was going to give him a bath, however, he turned around and ran off. Then I went looking for Rover.*

All of the necessary information for this passage is included in the paragraph, but the way that it is presented does not make sense. This story tells about a series of events involving washing a dog, so the best way to present the story would be in chronological order, meaning describing the events in the order in which they occurred. The proper order of this story should be:

> *It was Sunday afternoon, meaning it was time to give Rover, our dog, his weekly bath. I first went into the bathroom and filled the tub with water because I knew he wouldn't sit and wait quietly for me to fill it after I brought him into the bathroom. Then I went looking for Rover. At first, he ran right over to me when I called. When he realized that I was going to give him a bath, however, he turned around and ran off. I had to chase him around the house several times before I caught him.*

When the events of this story are presented in chronological order, the story as a whole makes more sense.

EXAMPLE 5

Read this passage, and then answer the question that follows.

The Frisbee is a flat, saucer-like flying disk toy that people toss back and forth to one another. It was invented in California in 1957 by a man named Walter Frederick at the height of the UFO (Unidentified Flying Object) craze. Frederick developed the flying disk, which resembled many people's description of UFOs as flying saucers.

He did not, however, call his invention a Frisbee. A company called Wham-O bought the rights to his flying saucer idea and then decided to name it after a popular restaurant in Bridgeport, Connecticut, which sold pies. The tins in which the pies were sold were saved by children after the pie was eaten, so they could toss them around. Thus, Frisbee's pies inspired the name of the flying disk: the Frisbee.

According to this passage, which of the following happened LAST?

Ⓐ   Wham-O named the flying disk the Frisbee.

Ⓑ   Walter Frederick invented a flying disk.

Ⓒ   Children tossed Frisbee pie tins around after eating the pies.

Ⓓ   Wham-O bought the rights to the flying disk.

First Frederick invented the disk, then Wham-O bought the rights. Children had been tossing Frisbee pies around for awhile, and when they heard about it, Wham-O decided to name their new toy after the restaurant.

Chapter 3

Comprehension and Analysis of Text

Author's Argument, Purpose, and Point of View

An author's **argument** is the primary subject and position that he or she is presenting in a written work. In some types of writing, the author's argument is easy to identify. For example, when a person writes a newspaper editorial, he or she usually states the issue to be addressed and his or her position on that issue. Then, an argument is presented.

Other times, though, the argument is not specifically stated and can be harder to figure out. This can often be seen in various forms of literature, including satire and fables. Satire is a type of writing that attacks some type of behavior, essentially arguing against it. A fable is a type of story that teaches a moral lesson, or argues in favor of a behavior. To determine the author's argument, you need to consider what he or she is discussing in the text and the message that he or she is trying to send.

EXAMPLE 1

The Frogs Ask for a King
from Aesop's Fables

The Frogs, upset by the fact that they had no established king, sent ambassadors to Zeus, the leader of the gods, asking for a king. Zeus, knowing that the Frogs were simple creatures, tossed a log down from the heavens, into the lake in which the Frogs lived. The Frogs, terrified by the log's splash, hid in the depths of the pool. When they realized that the log didn't move, they swam to it and climbed up on it.

Soon, they came to despise the log, considering themselves ill-treated by Zeus for sending them such an ineffectual leader. They decided to send a second delegation to Zeus asking him to send them another king. Bemused by the Frogs, he sent down an eel, which merely swam around in the lake. Again, the Frogs became dissatisfied with their leader and begged Zeus to send them a new king.

Finally, angry about their complaining, Zeus sent down a heron, which hunted the Frogs day by day, until there were none left to croak upon the lake.

What is the author arguing in this passage?

Ⓐ   Frogs need to change leadership frequently.

Ⓑ   Herons make the best leaders.

Ⓒ   It is better to have no leader than to have a cruel leader.

Ⓓ   It is better to have a cruel leader than no leader at all.

The author is arguing that it is better to have no leader than to have a cruel leader. When the Frogs did not have a leader, their only problem was that they were leaderless. When the heron was sent to them, it hunted and killed them.

Purpose refers to the reason why the author is writing. Writers generally write for one of three basic reasons: to educate, to entertain, or to persuade. When an author writes to educate, he or she presents information to expand the reader's knowledge. Types of writing written to educate include textbooks, encyclopedias, manuals, and nearly every other form of nonfiction writing. Literature is generally written to entertain the reader by telling him or her a story. Opinion pieces, such as newspaper editorials, are designed to persuade the reader to think a certain way.

All forms of writing have at least one purpose, and many have several. To determine the writer's purpose, think about what you as a reader get out of a text or passage. If it tells a story, it is likely designed to entertain. If it provides you with factual information, it is intended to educate you. If it presents an argument and valid evidence, it is trying to persuade you.

EXAMPLE 2

Read this passage, and then answer the question that follows.

The judicial branch of the government, also known as the court system, is responsible for interpreting the law. When the legislative branch creates a law, it is up to the executive branch to see that the law is carried out. When a person is accused of breaking the law, the judicial branch of government reviews the case and determines whether or not the person actually violated the law. In some special cases, the court may find that a law actually goes against the principles outlined in the U.S. Constitution. When this happens, the law is said to be unconstitutional, and it is struck down.

Why did the author write this passage?

Ⓐ   to entertain

Ⓑ   to educate

Ⓒ   to persuade

Ⓓ   to entertain, educate, and persuade

This passage was written to educate the reader about the judicial branch of government in the United States. It does not tell a story, so it is not intended to entertain, and it does not present an argument or take a position on an issue, so it is not designed to persuade.

Point of view refers to the perspective from which the writer is writing. Every person has his or her own personal perspective, which is influenced by lifestyle beliefs, experiences, social standing, religion, and countless other factors. When an author writes, the writing is affected by his or her personal point of view.

When you are aware of it, you can take what you know about the author into account when determining point of view. A male author, for example, might look at a situation from a man's point of view, whereas a female author might look at it from a woman's point of view. An author that you know holds certain beliefs or has had certain experiences will likely reflect them in his or her writing. For example, a book about war from a veteran would come from a different perspective than a book about war from a historian who has never spent a day in the military.

To determine an author's point of view, consider what the author is writing about, and the way in which he or she is writing. Often, if a writer is writing against something, he or she has had some negative experience with it. By the same token, someone writing in favor of something has likely had a positive experience with it.

EXAMPLE 3

> Joe Porter is running for mayor. He wants to lower city taxes, offer financial incentives to bring in new businesses, and increase the amount of downtown parking spaces. He also wants to reorganize city departments to save money and to improve the quality of services offered to citizens. Joe Porter would make a great mayor, and I think that everyone should vote for him.

What is the author's point of view in this passage?

(A)   The writer believes that the city should not have a mayor.

(B)   The writer believes that the city is not spending enough money.

(C)   The writer believes that city taxes are too low.

(D)   The writer believes that Joe Porter will improve the city.

From this passage, you can infer that the writer believes that Joe Porter will improve the city. The passage identifies several positive changes that Porter would make as mayor, each of which speaks to the writer's values. For example, he or she mentions that Porter will increase the amount of downtown parking and work to bring in new business. This indicates that the writer values economic prosperity, and that he or she feels new business is important to the city. Offering incentives and increasing parking availability for new customers would help to reach that goal.

Main Idea

The **main idea** of a text or passage is the basic message that the writer is trying to express to the reader. The most effective method of determining the main idea of a writing selection is identifying the topic sentence in each paragraph. The topic sentence establishes what the paragraph is about and is often located at the beginning of the paragraph, in the first or second sentence, although it can be anywhere in the paragraph, even as the last sentence in some cases. For example, read the following passage:

> *The American flag has a unique design. It consists of thirteen stripes, alternately red and white, and fifty white stars laid out on a field of blue in the upper left hand corner. The stripes represent the thirteen original colonies that first joined as the United States, and the stars represent each of the current fifty states. There is no known significance to the colors red, white, and blue. They were likely chosen since the flag of Great Britain, the country from which they declared their independence, used those three colors on its flag.*

The main idea of this passage is that the design of the Amercian flag is unique. It can be found in the topic sentence (the first sentence in this particular paragraph). While it contains other information, including specific design elements, every sentence connects to the main idea that the design of the flag is unique.

There will not always be a single topic sentence that captures the entire main idea of a passage. As a general rule, to determine the main idea, think about the basic message being imparted to the reader.

EXAMPLE 4

It was Saturday, the day Marvin had agreed to finally clean out the garage. He got up, went to the kitchen to have some coffee, and read the morning paper. In the paper, he noticed that the hardware store was having a sale. "It's only one day. I'd better get down there to pick up the circular saw I've been meaning to buy," he thought to himself. He went upstairs, shaved, showered and got dressed, then went down to the store.

While waiting in line to pay for his saw, Marvin noticed his friend, Stephen. The two struck up a conversation. Stephen was in the midst of building a deck that day and had stopped in to pick up some more screws. Marvin offered his assistance, and the two went off and spent the afternoon building the deck. Stephen asked Marvin if he'd like to go down to the local social club and watch the game. Marvin agreed, "Sure, but only for a little while, I still need to clean out the garage."

Marvin did not get home until later that evening. His wife, who had been out of town visiting her mother all day, came home soon after he did. "Did you manage to clean out the garage, dear?" she asked. Marvin replied, "You know how it is, I'm so busy this time of year. I'll clean it out next Saturday."

What is the MAIN IDEA of this passage?

Ⓐ   Marvin likes to build decks.

Ⓑ   Marvin enjoys shopping.

Ⓒ   Marvin does not like his wife.

Ⓓ   Marvin is easily distracted.

Marvin was unable to clean the garage because he kept allowing himself to be distracted into doing other things rather than clean the garage, which is what he was supposed to be doing.

Recognizing Supporting Details

After you have identified the topic sentence and/or main idea of a passage, you should be able to recognize supporting details that strengthen the argument regarding the main idea. For example,

> *Every summer my parents sent me to Camp Kanchigawokkie. I loved going to camp because I always had a great time there. I made new friends and together we did a lot of fun stuff. My favorite things to do were to go swimming, fishing, and hiking. Every night we had a campfire, roasted marshmallows, sang songs, and played games. While I was happy to see my family again at the end of the week, I was always a bit sad to leave.*

In this passage, the main idea is that the writer went to camp every year and had a good time. The supporting details are any details that back up this claim. So, supporting details in this passage include the fact that the writer made new friends, did a lot of fun stuff (such as swimming, fishing, and hiking), sang songs, and played games. Each of these statements relates directly to the main idea.

EXAMPLE 5

It was 8:45 and Duncan was running a little late. He stepped up to his car and reached into his pocket, but he found nothing there. That's when he realized he'd locked his keys in the car the night before.

A little upset, he rushed back into the house to find his extra set of keys. He looked on the key rack, but they weren't there. He checked his pants pockets and the sofa cushions, and he even went through the dirty laundry in the hamper. No luck—he just couldn't find them!

Feeling harried now, he grabbed a wire coat hanger and went back outside to try to pop open the lock. After struggling with it for a few minute she felt rain begin to fall. Unfortunately, he'd also locked himself out of the house, so he kept trying to get into his car. Eventually, the lock opened and he was able to get in. By the time he got to work, his hair was all wet and matted down, his suit was soaking wet, and he looked very sullen and unhappy.

The main idea of this story is that Duncan was having a bad morning. Which of the following details from the story MOST supports this statement?

Ⓐ   The man's name is Duncan.

Ⓑ   Eventually the lock opened and he was able to get in.

Ⓒ   Duncan was trying to get to work.

Ⓓ   Duncan got locked out of his car and was caught in the rain.

Getting locked out of his car and caught in the rain are the details which most support the claim that his having a bad morning is the main idea of the passage. While the other details are true, they do not directly support the main idea.

Drawing Inferences and Making Conclusions

An **inference** is a conclusion based on available information. In order to make an inference, you must have some form of evidence. For example, if you were walking home from school and suddenly smelled smoke and heard sirens, you would not need to see flames or the fire trucks to infer that there was a fire somewhere nearby. Your past experience and knowledge would lead you to that conclusion. An inference is your interpretation of the most likely conclusion based on the information made available to you at a particular moment.

You can draw inferences about:

- a character's personality, interests, or physical appearance
- a character's history
- a character's age
- the history of relationships between characters
- the reasons for specific character behaviors
- a character's intentions
- the next action a character will take

Remember, an inference is a conclusion based on available information—not a specific claim made directly within the passage.

EXAMPLE 6

Paul stood about 6' 4" and weighed well over 250 pounds. He had a deep voice with a thick Eastern European accent. An immigrant working as a miner, Paul was trying to earn enough money to bring the rest of his family to this country. He was generally considered a loner, keeping to himself in the boardinghouse where he rented a room. He never really socialized with anyone, and there were many rumors about where he'd come from and why he'd left.

From this passage, you can infer that Paul is

Ⓐ   six feet tall

Ⓑ   a miner

Ⓒ   intimidating

Ⓓ   from another country

Paul's large stature, deep voice, and heavy accent would likely make him an intimidating presence, although this is not specifically stated in the passage. Any information that is clearly stated cannot be an inference. Choice A is incorrect because the first sentence in the paragraph states that he is 6'4" tall. Choice B is incorrect because the paragraph clearly states that he is a miner. Choice D is incorrect because an immigrant is a person born in another country who comes to live here.

You should always be sure to read the passage carefully before trying to determine which choice is the proper inference. Read the passage, consider what inferences you can draw, and then look at the options to see if any of your first impressions are there.

Understanding Technical Instructions

Technical instructions are found in a technical manual or product manual. These are generally very straightforward and easy to follow because they are written to help readers locate information quickly and easily, not to try to teach them everything they need to know about the product or machine.

The instructions in a manual are often provided in a step-by-step format, which explains each individual action the reader should take to accomplish the task. To understand technical instructions, merely follow the directions.

EXAMPLE 7

This set of instructions came from a kitchen tabletop grill. Read through them and then answer the question that follows.

1. To operate the grill, first plug the power cord into an approved electrical outlet.

2. When you plug the cord in, the light on the top of the unit will turn on, indicating that the unit is on.

3. When the light turns off, the unit has reached its optimum temperature. At this point, you can begin cooking.

4. Open the top of the grill to expose the cooking surface. Be careful not to touch it, as it will be very hot.

5. Place the food on the grill and then close the lid. The unit will turn on and off as necessary to maintain the optimum cooking temperature.

6. Periodically check the unit while cooking to be sure that your food does not burn.

7. When finished, unplug the unit and set it aside to cool down before attempting to clean it.

What does it mean when the light on the unit shuts off?

Ⓐ   The unit has been plugged in.

Ⓑ   The food is done.

Ⓒ   The unit has reached optimum cooking temperature.

Ⓓ   The unit is broken.

According to step 3, when the light turns off, the unit has reached the optimum temperature.

Author's Evidence

Once the author has stated the argument, he needs to provide supporting evidence to prove his position. Just as supporting details are used to strengthen a claim about a passage's main idea, supporting evidence is used to back up a writer's argument in a persuasive piece. The two primary elements in such writing are

- fact vs. opinion
- bias and stereotype

Understanding Fact and Opinion

A **fact** is a statement whose validity, or truth, can be independently and objectively verified. For example, the statement "Indiana is a part of the United States" is a fact because it can be proven. By looking at a map you can see that Indiana is a state. By reviewing history books, state and federal documents, and newspaper articles, you can compile a great deal of evidence that proves Indiana is a state.

An **opinion** is an individual person's belief that may or may not be shared by others. For example, saying "chocolate cake makes the best birthday cake" would be expressing an opinion. Other people might feel that vanilla or strawberry cakes are better. A person with an allergy to chocolate might think that chocolate is the worst type of birthday cake. A clue that something is an opinion is if the statement talks about something being good or bad in some way. What is good to one person might be bad to another, and vice versa.

Another method of determining if something is an opinion involves looking for the use of superlatives (words that speak in extremes), such as *all, everyone, best,* and *worst.* When a writer uses superlatives, he or she is generally expressing an opinion, because it is often likely that one or more exceptions to the statement can be found. For example, you might write "she would never lie," but under certain circumstances she could lie, perhaps to avoid hurting someone's feelings or to protect someone she loves.

The same is true when a writer uses comparatives (words that suggest a comparison), such as *better, nicer,* or *smarter.* When a writer uses comparatives, he or she is almost always presenting an opinion.

Words that Often Indicate Opinions	
• always	• worst
• all	• no one
• never	• nobody
• bad	• none
• good	• every
• best	• everyone

EXAMPLE 8

Which of the following is a FACT?

Ⓐ   Julio is the funniest boy in class.

Ⓑ   The Earth is the third planet from our Sun.

Ⓒ   Nobody can run faster than I can.

Ⓓ   *Citizen Kane* is the best movie ever made.

Look for a well known, scientifically proven statement whose validity will not vary from person to person, as you find in choice B. You can often identify opinions in writing based on the use of comparative and superlative words, such as *better, best, worse,* and *worst.* Choices A and D are each opinions. For example, another person might think that Kevin is funniest boy in class and that *Casablanca* is a much better movie. Choice C would only be a fact if it could be proven that no one could, in fact, run faster than the writer.

EXAMPLE 9

Which of the following is NOT a factual statement?

Ⓐ   Women always like to shop more than men.

Ⓑ   Bears are usually covered with fur.

Ⓒ   Most automobiles have four wheels.

Ⓓ   Some people have trouble breathing at high elevations.

While some women like to shop more than some men, it is also true that some men like to shop more than some women. Choices B, C, and D can all be proven independently.

EXAMPLE 10

Which of the following is an OPINION?

Ⓐ   Everyone needs water to stay alive.

Ⓑ   The microscope allows us to see tiny organisms.

Ⓒ   Kids watch too much TV nowadays.

Ⓓ   Jupiter is a planet.

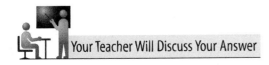
Your Teacher Will Discuss Your Answer

Recognizing Bias and Stereotype

Bias is an unfair preference for something, or an unfair dislike of something. A **stereotype** is an oversimplified image or trait assigned to an entire group by an individual. For example, if a person was sexist she would be *biased* against people of a specific sex. If that person believed that all of the people of that sex shared a common trait, that would be a stereotype.

A bias is a preference, and a stereotype is a belief. Biases are often based on belief of a stereotype.

To recognize bias or stereotype, consider whether the statements the writer makes are actually true, or if they are based on an oversimplified belief or an unjustified like or dislike of something. If there is not a valid reason to explain why the author feels a certain way about something, it is likely that the claim is the result of bias or stereotyping.

EXAMPLE 11

Which of the following statements indicates a bias?

Ⓐ   Dogs are just better than cats.

Ⓑ   Dogs will bark to let you know someone is at the door.

Ⓒ   Dogs are also known as canines.

Ⓓ   Cats are also known as felines.

Choice A indicates a preference for dogs over cats, but it does not provide any logical reason for the preference. It merely embraces dogs and dismisses cats.

EXAMPLE 12

Which of the following expressess a stereotype?

Ⓐ   We're going to call our soccer team *The Cougars*.

Ⓑ   Lorena wanted the guy with glasses to tutor her because people who wear glasses are smart.

Ⓒ   Football is played with an oddly shaped ball.

Ⓓ   Most people enjoy sweets, but eating them too often is unhealthy.

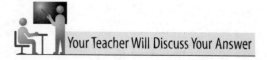
Your Teacher Will Discuss Your Answer

Selections for Practice

Selection 1

Lost!

We had been hiking through the woods all morning when it began to snow. At first, we didn't pay too much attention to the flakes that were falling as we continued onward. After an hour or so, though, we noticed that the snow was starting to fall faster and more heavily. In fact, it was starting to stick and accumulate.

Not exactly certain where we were or how we'd gotten there, the three of us stopped to figure out what we should do. Tommy wanted to keep moving forward. "We've got to be getting close to Parkerville," he said, referring to the town on the far side of the forest, opposite our own town, Burlington. "We should just keep walking until we get there, then we can call our parents to come pick us up."

"No," said Luther. "We should try to head back the way we came. The longer we wait, the harder it'll be to find the path we took. The snow is already starting to cover our tracks."

I didn't agree with either of them. We weren't sure where we were, and trying to go back the way we came or continuing to go the way we were headed could end up getting us even more lost. "I think we should make a shelter here and wait until the weather improves. Maybe we can even start a fire later, so anybody that comes looking for us will have an easier time finding us."

1a. Which character wanted to head back the way that they came?

- Ⓐ Tommy
- Ⓑ Luther
- Ⓒ the narrator
- Ⓓ all three characters

Go On

1b. **What town did the boys think they might be getting close to?**

Ⓐ Burlington

Ⓑ Parkerville

Ⓒ Indianapolis

Ⓓ Springfield

1c. **Information in this story is presented**

Ⓐ in reverse chronological order

Ⓑ from the viewpoint of each of the three characters

Ⓒ as a series of events

Ⓓ as a statistical summary

1d. **This passage is mostly about**

Ⓐ trying to figure a way out of a potentially dangerous situation

Ⓑ the dangers of sudden blizzards

Ⓒ the relationship between neighboring small towns

Ⓓ methods of survival

1e. **Which statement from the story expressess a FACT?**

Ⓐ We should make a shelter here and wait until the weather improves.

Ⓑ We've got to be getting close to Parkerville.

Ⓒ We should try to head back the way we came.

Ⓓ We noticed that the snow was starting to fall faster and more heavily.

Go On

Selection 2

I read an article in a magazine recently that described a man who had robbed a bank and stolen a car.

You probably didn't hear about this man's escapades. His story did not appear on the front page of your newspaper. No insurance claims were filed for the vehicles he destroyed. In fact, none of this really happened. It was all part of a video game.

Games such as the one described in this article are becoming increasingly common and more widely available to impressionable young people. At the same time, the rate of crimes committed by minors has also gone up dramatically. The severity of these acts is far more intense than at any other point in recent history, with some children and teenagers going to great lengths to commit crimes. Many people argue that there is no link between violent video games and criminal acts committed by minors, but the parallels are unmistakable.

In Appleton County, local law enforcement officers caught two boys attempting to steal an an older boy's car. When brought in for questioning, the boys explained that they were angry at the other boy for refusing to give them a ride to school several weeks before, and that they were planning to steal his car as revenge. Police believe that had the boys not been caught, the car would have been stolen and damaged.

Where did they get the idea to attempt such an act? In the aforementioned video game, in which the main character seeks revenge against enemies by stealing their cars. This is not a guess. The boys specifically told police that this was where they got the idea, and that they wanted to be "cool" like the criminal main character.

Video game producers need to step up and start taking some responsibility for the content to which they are exposing our nation's youth. The level of crime needs to be cut back extensively, and video game ratings must be more stringently enforced. Furthermore, parents need to be more aware of which games their children are playing, and what they are doing when they are not at home. If something is not done soon, the description I opened with will be a common newspaper article someday, and not just a game review.

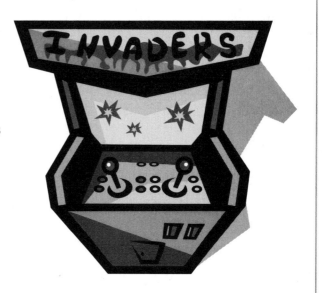

Go On

2a. Where did this passage MOST LIKELY appear?

    Ⓐ   textbook

    Ⓑ   instruction manual for a video game

    Ⓒ   editorial page of a newspaper

    Ⓓ   front page of a newspaper

2b. Complete the chart below by identifying how the video game described by the writer led to the actions taken by the boys.

Video Game Feature	Boys' Actions

2c. What is the author's point of view in this passage?

    Ⓐ   The writer believes that video game makers should reduce the level of crime in their games.

    Ⓑ   The writer believes that video game makers should be arrested for inciting crime.

    Ⓒ   The writer believes that parents should be arrested if their children commit crimes similar to those in video games.

    Ⓓ   The writer believes that children that commit crimes similar to those in video games should be punished more harshly than children that commit lesser types of crimes.

Go On

2d. The author wrote this passage PRIMARILY

    Ⓐ   to entertain and educate

    Ⓑ   to persuade and entertain

    Ⓒ   to educate and persuade

    Ⓓ   to entertain, educate, and persuade

2e. Identify TWO reasons the author gives to show that there is a connection between video game crime and real-life crime.

_____

_____

_____

2f. The author MOST LIKELY wrote this piece because

    Ⓐ   he wants to put video game makers out of business

    Ⓑ   he wants to increase awareness about the potential danger of violent video games that contain criminal activity

    Ⓒ   he thinks children do not understand that criminal acts hurt people and their possessions

    Ⓓ   he is not familiar with video games or crime

2g. Identify a bias of this author, and provide an example that supports your answer.

_____

_____

_____

Go On ➡

Selection 3

This set of instructions came with a rechargeable battery kit.

1. Plug the charging unit into a standard grounded wall outlet.

2. Insert the battery into the unit, matching the positive end of the battery to the positive end of the recharging chamber (match the + signs together on each piece).

   WARNING: NEVER insert into the unit any battery other than the original rechargeable battery that came with the unit. This unit is designed to be used ONLY with this battery, and may result in fire or explosion if a different battery is used.

3. When the battery is firmly in place, switch the dial on the unit to "Energy Level" to determine how much energy remains in the battery.

4. If the level is low, switch the dial to "Charge" and let the unit charge the battery for up to three hours.

5. When you are ready to remove the battery, switch the dial to "Off" and then take the battery out.

3a. Why shouldn't you put any other type of battery into this charger?

    Ⓐ   It would not charge properly.

    Ⓑ   It would invalidate the warranty.

    Ⓒ   It could cause a power failure.

    Ⓓ   It could cause a fire or explosion.

3b. On what setting should you place the unit to check how much power is still in the battery?

    Ⓐ   Off

    Ⓑ   Charge

    Ⓒ   Power On

    Ⓓ   Energy Level

STOP

Reading Comprehension

Unit 3 — Literary Response and Analysis

The Indiana Indicators addressed in this unit include:

7.3.1 Students should be able to discuss the purposes and characteristics of different forms of written text, such as the short story, the novel, the novella, and the essay.

7.3.2 Students should be able to identify events that advance the plot and determine how each event explains past or present action, or foreshadows future action.

7.3.3 Students should understand how to analyze characterization as shown through a character's thoughts, words, speech patterns, and actions; the narrator's description; and the thoughts, words, and actions of other characters.

7.3.4 Students should be able to identify and analyze themes—such as bravery, loyalty, friendship, and loneliness—which appear in many different works.

7.3.5 Students should understand how to contrast points of view—such as first-person, third-person, limited and omniscient, and subjective and objective—in narrative text and explain how they affect the overall theme of the work.

7.3.6 Students should be able to compare reviews of literary works and determine what influenced the reviewer.

GETTING the IDEA

A literary response is a written reaction to a book, play, or passage in which you present an argument about some aspect of the writing. Unit 3 discusses literary response to and analysis of different writing formats, including short stories, novels, novellas, and essays. This unit will help you to identify each of these types of writing by their unique characteristics.

Also discussed in Unit 3 are common elements of storytelling, including plot, character, theme, and point of view. You will learn the various elements of plot and how they are presented, as well as how to identify and analyze common themes, such as bravery, loyalty, friendship, and loneliness, that appear in many different works. You will also learn common methods by which authors reveal character, including analyzing characters' thoughts, words, speech patterns, and actions. The unit also reviews points of view, including first-person, third-person, limited, omniscient, subjective, and objective.

Finally, you will learn how to analyze critical works, such as book and movie reviews, to gain a deeper understanding of the writer's presentation.

Features of Literature: Narrative Analysis and Literary Criticism

Characteristics of Short Stories, Novels, Novellas, and Essays

There are many different formats authors can use when writing fiction. Each format has its own characteristics, advantages, and disadvantages. Some of the most common formats for fiction include short stories, novels, and novellas. In addition, authors write essays in which they critique, or analyze, works of fiction.

A **short story** is, as the name suggests, a story that does not take long to read. Characteristics of short stories include

- relatively small number of pages—A short story may range from less than a page up to a few dozen pages. Short stories are generally not published individually in book format. Instead, they appear as collections or as a part of some other medium (such as a magazine or journal).

- limited cast of characters—Because a short story is so short, there are generally only a handful of characters involved. There simply is not enough room to explore numerous characters.

- very focused plot—The plot of a short story is usually easy to determine early on because there is limited space in which to tell the story. Short stories generally begin with enough exposition for the reader to understand the plot and to identify the setting and characters.

- single plot—Unlike more developed and involved works, there is usually only one plot in a short story, as opposed to numerous plots and subplots.

- limited time span—The events in a short story usually take place in a limited amount of time, primarily because the plot is so focused and the work is so short.

The purpose of a short story is to tell a story in a relatively short period of time. Using the short story structure allows the writer to tell a tale that might not be developed enough or interesting enough to rate a full novel or novella. It also allows an author to make a point relatively quickly. The disadvantage of a short story is that it limits the degree to which the writer can describe events and characters, play out subplots, and expand upon the main plot.

A **novel** is a long work of fiction. Novels can take a long time to read and may be very involved. Characteristics of novels include

- length—There is no length limit on a novel, so they can range from a few hundred pages to potentially thousands of pages if the writer so chooses.
- published as single volumes—Novels are long enough to publish as a single volume.
- very developed plot—Because the writer is not limited by page count, he or she can create a very detailed, drawn-out plot that can take a long time to introduce, play out, and resolve.
- multiple plots and subplots—A novel may have more than one plot, and is likely to have several subplots, as the story is more involved and takes more time to tell.
- unlimited time span—A novel is a much longer story than a short story, and as such, it generally takes place over a much longer period of time, potentially over generations.

The purpose of a novel is to tell a long, detailed story that is fully developed, with rich descriptions of events, characters, and setting. The author can say whatever he or she wants to say without worrying about space constraints. The disadvantage of the novel format is that it is sometimes harder to get people to read it (because of the major time investment needed). Also, the reader can have greater difficulty identifying the main plot and keeping track of subplots and multiple characters because the work is so involved.

A **novella** is a written work that is longer than a short story, but not as long as a novel. Characteristics of novellas include

- intermediate length—Novellas are essentially short novels and are generally published as single volumes.
- larger cast of characters than a short story—There is more room to tell about more events and more people.
- more drawn-out plot than in a short story—While the plot is still relatively focused, in a novella, the writer has more time to build up to and expand upon the plot.
- use of subplots—Novellas may include multiple plots and/or subplots.
- longer time span than a short story—Again, because there is more room, the story can be told over a longer period of time.

The purpose of a novella is to tell a story too long for the short story format, but not as involved as a full novel. Using the novella format allows a writer to develop an idea or story further and to add multiple characters and sub-plots, without having to expand to a deeply involved novel format. The disadvantage of a novella is that the author cannot get as deeply involved in the story as he or she could with a novel.

An **essay** is a short piece of writing. Unlike short stories, novels, and novellas, essays are generally nonfiction critiques of literature or explanations of arguments. Characteristics of essays include

- short length—Essays often appear as journal or magazine articles.
- nonfiction material—Essays generally focus on fact and/or the writer's opinion, rather than tell a fictional story.
- presentation of an argument—Essays usually consist of the presentation of some form of argument and supporting evidence to back it up. In literature, essays are often used to present a critique of a short story, novel, or novella.

The purpose of an essay can vary, although the piece is generally a nonfiction presentation of ideas or arguments. In literature, essays often take the form of literary critiques in which the writer responds to a particular piece of writing or literary aspect (such as a genre or writing style). Essays are also used in other disciplines (areas of study), such as science and social studies, to present information and arguments.

EXAMPLE 1

Moby Dick **is an example of which type of writing?**

Ⓐ   short story

Ⓑ   novel

Ⓒ   novella

Ⓓ   essay

Moby Dick is a famous novel by Herman Melville about a man's hunt for a great whale. It is a long, thoroughly developed story featuring multiple plots and subplots and numerous characters.

EXAMPLE 2

"The Tell-Tale Heart" is an example of which type of writing?

Ⓐ   short story

Ⓑ   novel

Ⓒ   novella

Ⓓ   essay

"The Tell-Tale Heart" is a short story by Edgar Allan Poe. A good way to tell the difference between short works and long works by title is the way the title is written. Titles that are italized or underlined are generally titles of novels or novellas. Titles that appear in quotation marks are generally short stories or essays.

EXAMPLE 3

Which of the following would MOST LIKELY be an essay?

Ⓐ   "The Secret Life of Walter Mitty"

Ⓑ   <u>Oedipus Rex</u>

Ⓒ   "The Characterization of Women in the Works of Shakespeare"

Ⓓ   *The Adventures of Huckleberry Finn*

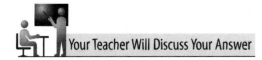

Your Teacher Will Discuss Your Answer

Understanding Plot

Plot is the main storyline in a narrative. It is what the story is about. The majority of the action in the story relates to the plot, and all of the main characters are somehow involved in it. It is characterized by the events that take place, with each important event somehow advancing it.

The important events in a plot do one of two things: They either explain past or present actions, or provide clues to future action (this is known as foreshadowing). For example, consider "Goldilocks and the Three Bears." The plot of this story is that a young girl, lost in the woods, goes into a house that she finds, uses the resources she finds there, then is chased away by the owners when they come home. The primary events in this story are

1. Girl gets lost and goes into a house.
2. Girl finds three bowls of porridge—the first is too hot, the second is too cool, but the third is just right.
3. Girl finds three chairs—the first is too hard, the second is too soft, but the third is just right.
4. Girl finds three beds—the first is too hard, the second is too soft, but the third is just right.
5. Owners come home and find their porridge eaten, their chairs sat in, and a girl sleeping in one of the beds.
6. Owners scare girl away.

Each of the first five events leads to the next event. For example, the girl would not find three bowls of porridge unless she went into the house. In this story, the events explain present action, although from time to time there might be mention of a past action in the story.

The story also includes foreshadowing. The reader quickly comes to understand that the next thing the girl finds will come in three varieties: two at opposite extremes, and one just right. The reader also knows that the bears are going to return, and that when they do, something important will happen.

EXAMPLE 4

Read this passage, and then answer the question that follows.

Jaguar
adapted from an ancient South American myth

In the ancient times, people ate their meat raw because they did not know how to make fire. Jaguar, the master of fire, ate his meat cooked. He was also a great hunter with bows and arrows, while man could do nothing but chase after animals on foot and hope to catch them.

Even though Jaguar was a very powerful being, he had a heart. He pitied the poor people who had to chase their food and eat it raw. One day, he came upon a hungry man in the jungle and took him home with him. There, he showed the man his fire, and he cooked some meat for him. The man, who had never eaten cooked meat, ate hungrily.

Then, Jaguar showed the man his weapons and taught him how to hunt with bows and arrows. Realizing his opportunity, the man used the weapons to kill Jaguar's wife, and then he stole his fire. Ever since then, humans have feared Jaguar, knowing he is out there in the jungle somewhere, hiding from people and waiting to take his revenge.

Why is Jaguar waiting to take revenge on man?

Ⓐ   Man has no fire.

Ⓑ   Man does not have bows and arrows.

Ⓒ   Man killed his wife and stole his fire.

Ⓓ   Jaguar is an evil creature.

Following the events of the story, you can see that first Jaguar had things that man did not, then he showed them to man. Next, man took Jaguar's things and killed his wife. For that reason, Jaguar is waiting to take revenge.

Understanding Character

Characterization refers to the author's description and development of a character in a story, including his or her appearance, behavior, beliefs, and so on. Writers can reveal character through

- the character's thoughts
- the character's words
- the character's speech patterns
- the character's actions
- the narrator's description
- the thoughts, words, and actions of other characters

Character's Thoughts

When the narrative style of a story allows the reader to "hear" a character's thoughts, it provides a greater insight into who the character is than any other factor. Nobody knows you better than yourself, and the same is generally true of characters in a story. Consider what the character is thinking, about herself and others, when developing your understanding of who the character is.

Character's Words

Similar to a character's thoughts, his words can give you an insight into who that person is, the experiences he has had, and what he believes. Keep in mind, though, that like real people, characters may not always say what they mean, and their words may differ from their actions.

Character's Speech Patterns

A character's speech patterns can give you certain insights into her personal background. An accent can indicate that a character comes from a certain part of the world. Poor grammar can be a sign of a lack of education. Very proper grammar, on the other hand, can indicate extensive schooling and/or coming from a socially advantaged group in which proper grammar is highly valued.

Character's Actions

Character can also be revealed by the way a person in a story acts. The things that a character does, either throughout the story or in a single significant act, can reflect that person's values. For example, if a character that acts cranky and mean throughout a story makes some sort of selfless sacrifice for others toward the end, that would indicate that his or her true character is kind and giving rather than mean and selfish.

Narrator's Description

In many stories, especially those which use a third-person, all-knowing (omniscient) point of view, the narrator's description of a character can be particularly relevant. The narrator can describe the character's physical appearance and provide details about the character's background that the reader otherwise might not be aware of. Always pay close attention to how the narrator talks about a character if you want to understand who that character really is.

Thoughts, Words, and Actions of Other Characters

The ways in which characters interact can also reveal character. Watch how different characters act around one another, how they treat one another, and the conversations that they have. Also pay attention to how characters talk or think about characters that are not present. The characters in a story often have known one another longer than the reader has been involved in the story, and their words and actions can reveal things that the reader would never know.

EXAMPLE 5

Read this passage, and then answer the questions that follow.

The three brothers, Bob, Paul, and Glen, were sitting at home on a rainy Saturday afternoon trying to figure out what they should do. "Let's get our toy cars and race them around in the kitchen!" said Bob.

"No, that's boring! I think we should play a game instead," replied Paul.

"I know! Let's play Parcheesi!" exclaimed Glen.

"I hate Parcheesi! I want to play cars!" cried Bob.

"Well, we hate cars, so we're gonna play a game," Paul said.

"Yeah, and we're gonna play checkers 'cuz that's a game for just two people, so you can't play!" added Glen.

Paul and Glen went off to play checkers while Bob went to get his toy cars. When he came back, he saw his brothers happily playing the game. When they told him to go away and stop watching them, he turned, picked up one of his cars, and threw it, hitting Glen in the head, causing him to cry.

"I hate you!" Glen said as the tears filled his eyes.

"I hate you, too!" Bob shouted back.

"I'm telling Mom!" Paul said, then he added, "and you're not our brother anymore!"

In this passage, Glen says, "Yeah, and we're gonna play checkers 'cuz that's a game for just two people, so you can't play!" From his speech patterns, you can tell that Glen is MOST LIKELY

Ⓐ   a farmer

Ⓑ   a schoolteacher

Ⓒ   a child

Ⓓ   a parent

The use of terms such as "gonna" and "'cuz" may reveal that the speaker is immature or speaking casually. The use of this type of language, called "colloquial," can sometimes mean the speaker is a child. From the other details in the story, along with this character's speech patterns, you can determine that Glen is in fact a child.

EXAMPLE 6

Refer to the passage in Example 5. Why did Paul say that Bob was not his brother anymore?

Ⓐ   Bob was adopted.

Ⓑ   Paul hates Bob.

Ⓒ   Paul hates Glen and Bob.

Ⓓ   Paul was angry with Bob for hurting his brother.

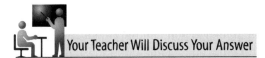 Your Teacher Will Discuss Your Answer

Theme

Theme refers to the central idea or meaning of a selection. It is the general idea or insight about life that an author wants the reader to understand. Theme differs from plot in that the plot of a story is what is happening with specific characters, while theme refers to the general message of the story.

A written work may have a single theme or several themes. Common literary themes include

- bravery—Courage in the face of real or perceived danger
- loyalty—Being faithful
- friendship—Often involves valuing a relationship over personal gain
- loneliness—Often involves the pain related to being on one's own
- love—Caring for another person, often even more than oneself
- greed—Valuing objects and riches over all else

To identify these and other themes in a passage, consider the actions, thoughts, and words of characters in the passage. When the characteristics of bravery, for example, are repeated several times in a story, you can determine that bravery is one of that story's themes.

EXAMPLE 7

Read this passage, and then answer the question that follows.

The Story of Della and Jim
adapted from "The Gift of the Magi" by O. Henry

Jim and Della were a happily married couple living in a modest home. Times were tough for this couple, and money was tight, but Christmas was coming and Della wanted to get something special for Jim. She had cut costs and pinched pennies throughout the year, but in those last few days before the holiday, she had only managed to come up with a dollar and eighty-seven cents. This was not nearly enough to buy the gift that she had hoped to be able to afford: a fancy chain for Jim's gold watch, which had been his father's and his grandfather's.

The only items of monetary value that the couple had were that watch and Della's hair. She had long, beautiful hair that was the envy of all who saw it. Long hair in and of itself was valuable because it could be used to make a wig, but hair as beautiful as Della's was considered especially valuable, as a hairpiece made of it could make the wearer look like an angel.

Understanding her situation, Della decided to sacrifice her hair so that she could buy her beloved the chain that she felt he truly deserved. She went and sold her hair, then bought the chain and brought it back to present to Jim. When he returned home that night, he was surprised and noticeably upset to find that his wife had cut off her hair. Thinking him angry with her, she sobbed and explained that she had had to sell her hair to be able to buy the wonderful gift for him, and she presented him with the chain.

He, in turn, presented her with a package, which she opened. Inside, she found a set of beautifully jeweled combs, which would have been perfect for running through Della's incomparable locks. She cried for a moment, then reminded Jim that her hair grows back so quickly. Then she gave him her present, which he opened and then smiled. "Let us put these gifts away for awhile. They're too nice to use right now."

Jim had sold his pocket watch to pay for the combs for Della's hair, just as Della had sold her hair to pay for the chain for Jim's pocket watch.

Which of the following is a theme in this passage?

Ⓐ   bravery

Ⓑ   greed

Ⓒ   loneliness

Ⓓ   love

The actions taken by Jim and Della were inspired by their love for one another. They each willingly gave up their most valuable possession to make their most valued person happier.

Point of View

Point of view refers to the perspective of the narrator. This differs from the perspective of the author in that the author is not always a character in a story, but every story has some form of narrator. The author is the person writing the story. The narrator is the person telling the story. The narrator may or may not be a character in the story, and the author may or may not agree with the narrator.

There are six main points of view in writing:

- first-person—Speaking from the personal ("I") point of view
- third-person—Speaking from an outside perspective (the narrator is not a character in the story)
- limited narration—The narrator does not know all the thoughts of all of the characters.
- omniscient narration—The narrator knows all thoughts of all characters.
- subjective—The point of view involves a personal perspective.
- objective—The point of view is from a distanced, informational perspective, such as in a news report.

First-Person

The first-person point of view can be seen in stories in which the narrator is a character. He tells the story from his personal point of view and often uses words such as *I*, *we*, and *us*. When a story is told in the first person, the reader's knowledge is limited to what can be told from the narrator's personal perspective.

First-person point of view affects the overall theme of a work. Since you are only exposed to the narrator's point of view, you are generally limited to seeing things as he sees them. You do not get to "hear" the thoughts of other characters, nor are you told what characters are doing when the narrator is not around. This can make it harder to determine what the theme is.

Third-Person

Third-person point of view is the perspective of someone who is usually not directly involved in the story. The word *I* is rarely used by third-person narrators because the narrator is only telling the story, not taking part in it.

Third-person point of view can make it easier to identify the theme of a story because the reader is exposed to the thoughts and feelings of multiple characters and can observe how certain characters act when other characters are not around. However, it is important to note that third-person point of view can take several forms, including limited point of view, omniscient point of view, subjective point of view, and objective point of view. While each of these can technically be a form of third-person point of view, they have their own distinct qualities that set them apart from one another.

Limited

In stories told in limited point of view, the narrator does not know all the thoughts of all characters. First-person point of view is a type of limited narration because the narrator knows only his own thoughts, but third-person point of view can also be limited if there are one or more characters who are a mystery to the narrator.

Limited point of view affects the theme of a story by revealing only some characters' thoughts and feelings, leaving the reader to interpret the thoughts and feelings of other characters.

Omniscient

Omniscient point of view is the most common form of third-person point of view. With this point of view, the narrator knows everything about all characters and events. Omniscient point of view makes it easier to identify theme because the reader understands the motives of different characters, making it easier to understand why people do what they do.

Subjective

The subjective point of view involves a personal perspective on the narrator's part. First-person point of view almost inherently includes the narrator's perspective, but third-person point of view can also be subjective. The narrator may have an agenda or may have certain feelings about certain characters that he or she does not hide.

Subjective point of view can affect theme by slightly twisting the events of a story to fit the narrator's beliefs. What the reader sees may not be entirely accurate, and characters may not be exactly what they are portrayed to be.

Objective

The objective point of view does not allow the narrator's own thoughts and feelings to affect the storytelling. Events and characters are described exactly as they are, meaning the reader can take the narrator at his or her word. Objective point of view can make it easier to identify theme in that the reader can rely on what the narrator says; but by the same token, without subjective point of view, the reader may not be made aware of certain qualities or actions of other characters.

EXAMPLE 8

Which of the following sentences uses first-person narration?

Ⓐ   It was hard to work with a person like that.

Ⓑ   I thought he was going to go, but at the last minute, he decided not to.

Ⓒ   He left to go to the store, but he never came back.

Ⓓ   He was feeling sad about leaving, but he knew he had to go.

Look for the sentence in which the narrator is a character in the story and refers to himself. Choice A is considered subjective, Choice C is third-person, and Choice D is omniscient.

EXAMPLE 9

In limited point of view, the narrator knows the thoughts and feelings of

Ⓐ   one character

Ⓑ   two to four characters

Ⓒ   all characters

Ⓓ   one or several, but not all characters

Even if a story has a hundred characters, if there is one character whose thoughts and feelings are not known by the narrator, then point of view is limited. The narrator knows the thoughts and feelings of all characters when using the omniscient point of view.

EXAMPLE 10

In which point of view does the narrator include his or her opinion of events or characters?

Ⓐ   limited

Ⓑ   omniscient

Ⓒ   subjective

Ⓓ   objective

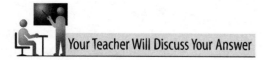 Your Teacher Will Discuss Your Answer

78

EXAMPLE 11

In which type of writing would you **MOST LIKELY** find objective point of view?

Ⓐ   short story

Ⓑ   novel

Ⓒ   poem

Ⓓ   news report

News reports are supposed to be objective, meaning they focus only on the facts.

Critical Analysis

A **critical analysis** examines a written piece and determines why the author was affected the way she was. A common form of critical analysis is the review. You probably encounter reviews on a pretty regular basis. Movies, books, albums, plays, and concerts are often reviewed in the newspaper, on television, on the radio, or online.

To analyze a review, consider what the reviewer is saying, and then try to determine why the writer was affected in that way. For example, read the following movie review:

> *Director Alan Dodd has done it again. His latest masterpiece, <u>Daylight</u>, features suspense, action, intrigue, and an ample amount of dark humor. Fans of his previous films, including <u>Undersea</u> and <u>Diogenes</u>, will be thrilled to see that the master has not lost his touch. Fans of gothic horror and political intrigue will thrill to the twists and turns of Dodd's story of a man on a journey to the center of his soul. <u>Daylight</u>, simply put, is one of the best feature films of the year. Don't miss it!*

The first thing you should do when looking at this piece is to determine what the writer's feeling about the work was. In this instance, you can tell that the writer enjoyed the movie because she uses positive language such as "masterpiece", "thrilled", and "best feature film of the year".

Next, consider why the writer feels the way she does. To do so, focus on the positive aspects of the film mentioned by the writer, and think about what she values. The writer's values will be reflected in her opinion. For example, the author mentions suspense, action, intrigue, and dark humor in a positive way. This indicates that the writer enjoys these qualities in a movie. If the reviewer was a big fan of just romance films, for example, she would probably not enjoy this movie.

She also refers to the director as a "master" and to the movie as a "masterpiece". These references indicate that the reviewer is a fan of this particular director, meaning she was likely biased in favor of the movie even before seeing it.

As with any type of writing, the best way to determine why the author wrote what she did is to think critically about what was written, and then try to determine what influenced the author.

EXAMPLE 12

Read this sample book review, and then answer the questions that follow.

> Anne Wellington, known for her epic tales of struggle and survival, departs from her standard writing style in her latest book, ***Woodchuck Falls***. This novel tells the story of a man and a woman who were childhood friends, then were separated when each family moved to a different part of the country. The two are unexpectedly reunited in a small town called Woodchuck Falls as each happens to be passing through. Wellington's latest story starts off strong but quickly lulls into standard love-story tripe involving numerous cliches and overly pat resolutions. I had expected more from this author, whose previous works were innovative and deeply engaging, but this time she seems to go for the easy out, refusing to challenge herself or the reader. True fans of this writer will want to avoid this book, if only to prevent themselves from tarnishing their mental image of her.

How does the reviewer feel about this book?

Ⓐ   likes it

Ⓑ   dislikes it

Ⓒ   has no opinion of it

Ⓓ   cannot make up his or her mind

The reviewer uses negative language and speaks of the book and writer in less than flattering terms. Therefore, he seems to dislike this book.

EXAMPLE 13

Refer to the review in Example 12. Why do you think the reviewer did not like the book?

Ⓐ   The reviewer probably does not like any books.

Ⓑ   The reviewer is temperamental.

Ⓒ   The reviewer thought the book should have been much longer.

Ⓓ   The reviewer was expecting a book similar to the author's previous works.

The reviewer mentions the author's previous novels and speaks of this current book in negative terms in comparison to the others, suggesting that choice D is the correct answer.

Unit 3

Selections for Practice

Selection 1

My Grandfather's Clock

by Henry Clay Work

1	My grandfather's clock was too large for the shelf,
2	So it stood ninety years on the floor;
3	It was taller by half than the old man himself,
4	Though it weighed not a pennyweight more.
5	It was bought on the morn of the day that he was born,
6	And was always his treasure and pride;
7	But it stopped short never to go again
8	When the old man died.
9	[Chorus] Ninety years, without slumbering (tick, tick, tick, tick)
10	His life seconds numbering (tick, tick, tick, tick)
11	It stopp'd short never to go again
12	When the old man died.
13	[Solo] In watching its pendulum swing to and fro,
14	Many hours had he spent while a boy;
15	And in childhood and manhood the clock seemed to know
16	And to share both his grief and his joy,
17	For it struck twenty-four when he entered at the door,
18	With a blooming and beautiful bride;
19	But it stopped short never to go again
20	When the old man died.
21	[Chorus] Ninety years, without slumbering (tick, tick, tick, tick)
22	His life seconds numbering (tick, tick, tick, tick)
23	It stopp'd short never to go again
24	When the old man died.

Go On

Literary Response and Analysis

25 [Solo] My grandfather said that of those he could hire,
26 Not a servant so faithful he found;
27 For it wasted no time, and had but one desire—
28 At the close of each week to be wound.
29 And it kept in its place—not a frown upon its face,
30 And its hands never hung by its side;
31 But it stopped short never to go again
32 When the old man died.

33 [Chorus] Ninety years, without slumbering (tick, tick, tick, tick)
34 His life seconds numbering (tick, tick, tick, tick)
35 It stopp'd short never to go again
36 When the old man died.

37 [Solo] It rang an alarm in the dead of the night—
38 An alarm that for years had been dumb;
39 And we knew that his spirit was pluming for flight—
40 That his hour of departure had come.
41 Still the clock kept the time, with a soft and muffled chime,
42 As we silently stood by his side;
43 But it stopped short never to go again
44 When the old man died.

45 [Chorus] Ninety years, without slumbering (tick, tick, tick, tick)
46 His life seconds numbering (tick, tick, tick, tick)
47 It stopp'd short never to go again
48 When the old man died.

1a. **This poem is told from which point of view?**

Ⓐ first-person

Ⓑ third-person

Ⓒ omniscient

Ⓓ objective

Go On

1b. Which of the following is a theme in this passage?

    Ⓐ   building clocks

    Ⓑ   having grandchildren

    Ⓒ   passage of time

    Ⓓ   inheriting possessions

1c. "My Grandfather's Clock" is CLOSEST in style to which of the following?

    Ⓐ   short story

    Ⓑ   novel

    Ⓒ   essay

    Ⓓ   novella

1d. The narrator implies that the clock stopped working because

    Ⓐ   it was not well cared for

    Ⓑ   the narrator's grandfather died

    Ⓒ   it was too old to run any longer

    Ⓓ   it was destroyed in an accident

Go On

Literary Response and Analysis

Selection 2

Ol' Charlie

Nobody in our platoon really liked ol' Charlie. Well, nobody but me, that is. I don't know why, really, but there was something about Charlie that just seemed so darn likeable to me. None of the other guys thought so, though. They all thought he was too interested in himself because he didn't hang out with the guys like everybody else did. When we weren't fighting the enemy, he was spending his time pretty much alone, reading whatever he could find or writing in that journal of his.

Camaraderie is a pretty important thing in the military, especially to guys like us who were fighting on the front lines. Out there, you have to depend on your buddies to watch your back, or else you'll end up getting yourself shot. The problem is, most of the guys didn't think about Charlie as one of their buddies. And if he wasn't a buddy, then he was a liability. That meant that if you were relying on Charlie to watch your back, you were as good as dead. At least that's what they thought. I didn't think so, though.

Then one day during a firefight, it happened. Somehow, our group had gotten surrounded by the enemy, and there was no way out. We formed a circle and were firing back at them, trying our best to fend 'em off. Deep in our hearts, though, there wasn't a man in that circle who didn't think his time was just about up. But only one of us was right.

When you're surrounded on all sides by an enemy, your only hope of getting out is to break a hole in their line and then push on through. We were just too overwhelmed to think straight, though. And I'm not ashamed to admit it, some of us were just too plain scared. The only guy who really had his head on straight that day was ol' Charlie.

I remember him stepping back into the center of our circle, with some of the guys screaming at him, calling him a chicken. They didn't understand what he was doing, though. He reached over and pulled the grenades off my vest, and did the same to a few other guys on either side of me. Then he looked out toward the enemy and found what he figured to be the weakest point, and he lobbed a grenade at 'em.

That first blast caught 'em by surprise, and the shooting from that side stopped for a moment. Charlie didn't, though. He broke through the circle, lobbing grenade after grenade in that direction, running directly into the line of fire, just to open up the line for us. Just to give us a chance to get out of there. Just to give us a chance to survive.

We did survive. After the second grenade blast, our guys made a break for the hole, and we made it through and were able to escape. Unfortunately, ol' Charlie didn't make it. Yessir, I always said they were all wrong about ol' Charlie.

Go On

2a. This passage is an example of which type of writing?

    Ⓐ   novel

    Ⓑ   novella

    Ⓒ   essay

    Ⓓ   short story

2b. Which of the following is a theme in this passage?

    Ⓐ   greed

    Ⓑ   selflessness

    Ⓒ   hatred

    Ⓓ   loneliness

2c. Why did Charlie launch his one-man attack against the enemy?

    Ⓐ   He hated the enemy.

    Ⓑ   He was a double agent.

    Ⓒ   He wanted to give his platoon a chance to escape.

    Ⓓ   He was frightened and was trying to get away.

Go On

2d. Identify TWO ways in which the author reveals character in this passage.

_____

_____

_____

2e. Identify TWO points of view used in this narration, and provide a reason to support each answer.

_____

_____

_____

Selection 3

Movie Review

In a world where money means everything, sometimes the best things in life are free. From award-winning director Jeremy McClintock comes *Diamonds in the Grass*, a story of love, friendship, and triumph over adversity. This is a fantastic movie featuring all of the classic film elements woven together into a timeless tale that will continue to fascinate audiences for years to come. The acting is top-notch, the cinematography is dazzling, and the musical score is hauntingly beautiful. *Diamonds in the Grass* is appropriate for all people of all ages, so it should not be missed by anyone. See *Diamonds in the Grass*, now playing at the Bijou Theatre downtown. You won't be disappointed.

3. Identify the reviewer's reaction to the movie *Diamonds in the Grass*, and give TWO examples that support his or her opinion of the film.

_____

_____

_____

_____

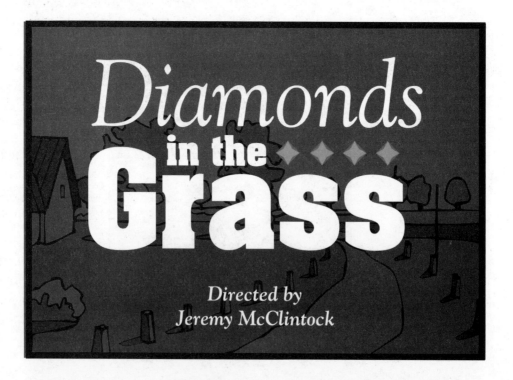

Literary Response and Analysis

Unit 4
Written English Language Applications

The Indiana Indicators addressed in this unit include:

7.6.1 Students should be able to properly place modifiers and use the active voice when wishing to convey a livelier effect.

7.6.2 Students should understand how to identify and use infinitives and participles.

7.6.3 Students should be able to make clear references between pronouns and antecedents by placing the pronoun where it shows to what word it refers.

7.6.4 Students should be able to identify all parts of speech and types and structure of sentences.

7.6.5 Students should understand how to demonstrate appropriate English usage.

7.6.6 Students should understand how to identify and correctly use hyphens, dashes, brackets, and semicolons.

7.6.7 Students should be able to demonstrate the correct use of quotation marks and the use of commas with subordinate clauses.

7.6.8 Students should be able to use correct capitalization.

7.6.9 Students should be able to correctly spell derivatives by applying the spelling of bases and affixes.

GETTING the IDEA

Now that you know how important it is to be able to understand what you have read, you should understand the importance of using words and sentences correctly in your own writing so that others will be able to understand what you are trying to say.

Unit 4 examines the important points of sentence structure, grammar, punctuation, and capitalization, including using modifiers, active voice, infinitives, participles, pronouns and antecedents, quotation marks, commas, semicolons, colons, hyphens, dashes, capital letters, prefixes, suffixes, and roots.

In order to write effectively, you must also be able to identify and correctly use modifiers (words or phrases that describe, limit, or qualify another word), infinitives (the *to* form of a verb), participles (the *–ing* form of a verb), and pronouns (words substituted for nouns). You should also understand how to write in the active voice to make your writing livelier and more interesting.

Once you know which words to use and how to use them, you need to understand the other elements that affect sentence structure, such as punctuation (marks used to indicate shifts of different kinds in sentences) and proper capitalization (when and where to use capital letters).

Finally, Unit 4 identifies common prefixes, suffixes, and roots which will help you to learn what alternate forms of common words mean as well as how to spell them correctly.

Chapter 5 Sentence Structure and Grammar

Using Modifiers

A **modifier** is a word or phrase that gives information about another word or phrase and may describe, limit, or qualify another word. For example,

> We have <u>only</u> one cat.

In this sentence, the word *only* is the modifier. It limits the number of cats we have to one. Without *only*, the sentence would read,

> We have one cat.

This could be interpreted to mean that we have only one cat, but it could also mean that we have at least one cat, and possibly more.

Always be sure that the modifier you are using clearly modifies the proper word. Failure to do so changes the meaning of the sentence. For example,

> **Clear:** *The boy that had been left behind sat on the park bench.*

> **Unclear:** *The boy sat on the park bench that had been left behind.*

In the second sentence, the writer seems to indicate that the bench, rather than the boy, had been left behind. When the modifier is placed correctly, there is no confusion as to the true meaning of the sentence.

EXAMPLE 1

You have to take two tests at school today. Which of the following sentences expresses this thought?

Ⓐ   I have to take some tests today at school.

Ⓑ   I have tests at some school today.

Ⓒ   At school, I have many tests today.

Ⓓ   I have no tests today.

In the correct sentence the modifier *some* means more than one, but not all that many, and in this sentence, it is properly placed next to *tests*, the word which it modifies. Choice B indicates that tests may be taken at one of several schools. Choice C indicates that there are far more than two tests to be taken, and choice D implies that tests will not be taken today.

Using Active Voice

Active voice refers to the form of the verb indicating that the subject is doing the action. **Passive voice** is the form of the verb indicating that the subject is the receiver of the action. For example,

> **Active voice:** *Donna <u>bought</u> ice cream for all of the children.*

> **Passive voice:** *The children's ice cream <u>was bought</u> by Donna.*

In the first sentence, the subject is *Donna*, and she is actively buying the ice cream for the children. In the second sentence, the subject is *ice cream*, and it receives the action of the verb *was bought*.

Using active voice makes writing livelier and more interesting to read. It is more engaging for the reader, as opposed to passive voice, which takes emphasis away from the doer of the action.

To identify whether a sentence uses the active or passive voice, first determine what the subject of the sentence is. Next, consider whether the subject performs the action of the verb, or whether it receives the action of the verb (is acted upon). If the subject is engaging in some action, the sentence is using the active voice. If the subject is receiving the action, the sentence is written in the passive voice.

Sentences with verbs written in the present tense, the present participle, or the past tense are generally active voice sentences. When the verb is given in the past participle, the sentence is sometimes a passive voice statement.

EXAMPLE 2

Which of the following sentences uses active voice?

Ⓐ   The book was brought by Don.

Ⓑ   The parakeet was fed by Hannah.

Ⓒ   The calendar had been printed by a company in Canada.

Ⓓ   Karen is singing like an angel.

The subject of choice D is *Karen*, and the action is *is singing*. In the other sentences, the subjects receive the actions of the verbs.

EXAMPLE 3

Which of the following sentences uses passive voice?

Ⓐ   Earl and Warren are forming their own rock band.

Ⓑ   The crate was carried in yesterday by the deliverymen.

Ⓒ   The little girl is crying because she can't find her doll.

Ⓓ   Nobody wants you to leave.

The subject of choice B is *crate*, and it receives the action of the verb *was carried*. The other sentences involve the subject actively doing something.

Using Infinitives and Participles

An **infinitive** is a verb phrase consisting of *to* followed by the base form of a verb. For example, the base form of the verb *running* is *run*, so the infinitive version is *to run*.

Infinitives can function as

- subject of a sentence—To act is my life's ambition.
- direct object—I love to dance.
- adjective—She lacked the desire to go.
- adverb (function is usually to tell why)—We came to apologize.

EXAMPLE 4

Which word or phrase best completes this sentence?

Sometimes I just need _____ about things.

Ⓐ thinking

Ⓑ think

Ⓒ to think

Ⓓ to thought

Adding *to* to the root form of the verb *think* creates *to think*. This sentence requires the use of an infinitive.

EXAMPLE 5

In which sentence does the infinitive act as the subject of a sentence?

Ⓐ I want to write.

Ⓑ She asked to go.

Ⓒ It is fun to sing with others.

Ⓓ To speak is to be heard.

In choice D, *to speak* is the subject. It is what the sentence is about.

A **participle** is a verb which has –<u>ing</u>, –<u>d</u>, –<u>ed</u>, –<u>n</u>, –<u>en</u>, or –<u>t</u> added to the base form of the verb. For example, participles of *dream* would be *dreaming*, *dreamed*, and *dreamt*.

There are two basic types of participles

- present participle—Happening now (ending in –<u>ing</u>); Joe <u>is singing</u>.
- past participle—Had happened earlier (usually consists of <u>had</u> + past tense form, although there are some exceptions); Joe <u>had sung</u>.

Participles are often used as

- adjectives that describe a noun—The <u>jogging</u> man tripped and fell.
- parts of a verb phrase—They <u>are riding</u> their bikes to town.

EXAMPLE 6

Which word or phrase BEST completes this sentence?

Don't worry, the judge _____ your record because you are a minor.

Ⓐ   seals

Ⓑ   is sealing

Ⓒ   had sealed

Ⓓ   had sealing

Choice B requires the use of a present participle, which is part of the verb phrase *is sealing*.

EXAMPLE 7

In which of the following sentences is a participle used as part of a phrase?

Ⓐ   I am going to the store.

Ⓑ   That is an intriguing offer.

Ⓒ   You are an interesting person.

Ⓓ   Driving is important to me.

In choice A, the verb phrase is *am going*. Choices B and C use participles as adjectives, and choice D uses the participle as the subject of the sentence.

Pronouns and Antecedents

A **pronoun** is a word that takes the place of a noun and functions as a noun. Pronouns are used as a sort of shortcut that allows you to refer to a noun without repeating the noun over and over again.

Common Pronouns		
he	him	his
she	her	hers
they	them	their
you	your	yours
we	us	our
I	me	my
it	its	

Because pronouns are substitutes for nouns, they generally have to refer to a previously used noun. The noun that the pronoun replaces is known as the **antecedent**. When using pronouns with antecedents, you must always be sure that the appropriate pronoun is used. This is known as pronoun-antecedent agreement.

ISTEP+ Coach, English/Language Arts, Level G

In order for the pronoun and antecedent to agree, they must match in gender and number. If the antecedent is masculine, the pronoun should be masculine. If the antecedent is singular, the pronoun should be singular, and so on. To be sure that the two agree, first identify the antecedent, then use the appropriate pronoun replacement. For example,

> *Joe went to Joe's house.*

Forms of the word *Joe* appear twice in this sentence, so you would want to replace the second appearance with a pronoun. The antecedent is *Joe*, which is masculine and singular, so you would replace it with a masculine, singular pronoun. The correct way to revise this sentence is

> *Joe went to his house.*

EXAMPLE 8

What is the best way to rewrite this sentence?

> Danny and Marie are going to drive Danny and Marie's car to the party.

Ⓐ   Danny and Marie are going to drive my car to the party.

Ⓑ   Danny and Marie are going to drive her car to the party.

Ⓒ   Danny and Marie are going to drive us car to the party.

Ⓓ   Danny and Marie are going to drive their car to the party.

The subject of the sentence is "Danny and Marie," which is plural (because it involves more than one person). The phrase being replaced, "Danny and Marie's," is possessive, meaning that it shows ownership, so the pronoun should be possessive. The best plural possessive pronoun in this case, then, is *their*.

As when using modifiers, you need to be careful when using pronouns to ensure that the message you send is clear. For example,

> *Carol told Susan that Susan was a wonderful painter.*

At first glance, you would think that the second *Susan* can simply be replaced with *she*. Consider the meaning of the new sentence when doing this, though.

> *Carol told Susan that she was a wonderful painter.*

96

NOTICE: Photocopying any part of this book is forbidden by law.

This sentence can be interpreted to mean that Carol thinks that Susan is a wonderful painter or that Carol thinks that Carol is a wonderful painter. When replacing the pronoun would result in an unclear sentence, some rewriting is necessary. A good way to rewrite this sentence without changing its meaning is

Carol told Susan, "You are a wonderful painter."

When using pronouns, always double check to make sure that the replacement sentence means what the original sentence meant.

EXAMPLE 9

What is the best way to rewrite this sentence?

Janet thought that Wanda did not want to go to Janet's party.

Ⓐ Wanda thought that Janet did not want to go to her party.

Ⓑ "I don't think Wanda wants to come to my party," Janet thought.

Ⓒ Janet thought that Wanda did not want to go to their party.

Ⓓ Janet thought that Wanda did not want to go to her party.

 Your Teacher Will Discuss Your Answer

Punctuation and Capitalization

Punctuation

Punctuation refers to the special marks used in writing to accentuate something, indicate a pause or an end, or indicate some special feature about a phrase or numbers. The most common forms of punctuation include

- quotation marks
- commas
- semicolons
- colons
- hyphens and dashes

Quotation Marks

Quotation marks look like a pair of apostrophes ("). They are most commonly used to enclose the exact words of a speaker. For example,

"Do you want to go to the park?" asked Ronald.

Ronald's exact words are "Do you want to go to the park," so the quotation marks appear around that phrase.

When using quotation marks in this way, you also have to be careful about the punctuation at the end of the sentence being spoken. Unless the spoken phrase ends in a period (.), the regular punctuation is used. If the spoken phrase would normally end in a period, though, the period should be replaced with a comma, unless it indicates the end of the entire sentence. For example,

"Look at all the snow!" exclaimed Velma.

Because the spoken phrase would normally end with an exclamation point, it can remain an exclamation point. However, read this sentence.

"I think we should plant flowers." said Jude.

The period at the end of "I think we should plant flowers" would need to be replaced with a comma. In other words, you don't want two periods within the same sentence. The correct way to write this sentence is

"I think we should plant flowers," said Jude.

Now let's say that the order of this sentence were reversed. In this case, the spoken phrase (rather than "said Jude") is at the end of the sentence, so it would be written like this:

Jude said, "I think we should plant flowers."

You'll also notice that a comma was added after "Jude said" this time. This is done to indicate a transition between the subject's action and the words being spoken.

Quotation marks are also used around the titles of

- articles
- poems
- songs
- short stories
- chapters in books

This means that you would use quotation marks when writing the name of any of these types of writing. For example,

I read an article entitled "How to Use Punctuation Properly" in today's newspaper.

My favorite poem is "I Wandered Lonely as a Cloud."

Let's all sing "Happy Birthday" together!

Tonight I will read "Dissertation on Roast Pig" before going to bed.

Turn your books to Chapter 4, "Native Americans in U.S. History."

EXAMPLE 1

Choose the sentence that shows the correct punctuation.

Ⓐ   "The cabinet is made of mahogany." stated Arnold.

Ⓑ   Chuck said, "This is a book about penguins,"

Ⓒ   "Here we go again!" exclaimed Rupert.

Ⓓ   "Are you sure," asked Jamie.

The quotation marks are used around the exact sentence that Rupert said, and since the comment ends in an exclamation point rather than a period, it remains an exclamation point. The period after *mahogany* in choice A should be a comma. The comma at the end of choice B should be a period, and the comma after *sure* in choice D should be a question mark.

EXAMPLE 2

Which of the following should you put quotation marks around?

Ⓐ   name of a book

Ⓑ   name of a person

Ⓒ   name of a song

Ⓓ   all of the above

Quotation marks should be used around the names of songs, articles, short stories, chapters in books, and poems. The title of a book is italicized or underlined, and no special punctuation should be used for a person's name.

Commas

A comma (,) is a special kind of punctuation that is used to indicate a transition or separation in writing. Commas are used before a conjunction when linking two sentences, ideas, or phrases; after introductory words or phrases; and to separate items in a series.

When used with subordinate clauses, commas are used to separate the subordinate clause from the main clause.

Although he didn't want to Jimmy agreed to go.

In this sentence, the main clause is "Jimmy agreed to go" and the subordinate clause is "although he didn't want to." When written without a comma, the sentence does not make any sense because the subordinate and main clauses are joined together. In order to clarify this sentence's meaning, a comma should be added between the two clauses, like so:

Although he didn't want to, Jimmy agreed to go.

You'll notice that the comma is used when subordinate clauses begin the sentence. A sentence beginning with a subordinate clause—*because, if, when, after,* etc.—is usually a clue that a comma is needed.

Because he was ill, Ricardo stayed home.

After you dust, please vacuum as well.

EXAMPLE 3

Choose the sentence that shows the correct punctuation.

Ⓐ When I wake up tomorrow I will call you.

Ⓑ Even if she does, we won't know right away.

Ⓒ As hard as, he tried, he always failed.

Ⓓ While driving, to work, I saw, a deer.

The comma belongs between the subordinate and main clauses. Choice A is incorrect because it needs a comma after *tomorrow*, and choices C and D are incorrect because they have too many unnecessary commas.

Semicolons

A semicolon (;) looks like a combination of a colon and a comma. Like commas, semi-colons are used to indicate a transition. Unlike commas, though, when they are being used to link two different sentences or phrases, they may be used if there is <u>not</u> a conjunction. For example,

> *Some basketball players are tall; others are not.*

If the sentence was written with a conjunction such as *but*, you would use a comma ("Some basketball players are tall, but others are not."). However, since there is no conjunction, a semicolon is used.

Semicolons are used when certain subordinating conjunctions join sentences.

> *I saved my allowance for weeks; therefore, I could afford the dress.*

Semicolons are also used when making a list, but only if the items in the list include commas. For example,

> *Tula ordered a hamburger, fries, and orange juice; Sam ordered a sandwich, potato chips, and tea; and Seth ordered roast duck, mashed potatoes, and some ice water.*

A good general rule of thumb is that commas are used for lists, and semicolons are used for lists of lists.

EXAMPLE 4

Where would you place the semicolon in this sentence?

> We do not have much time I think we can make it.

Ⓐ   after the first *we*

Ⓑ   after *have*

Ⓒ   after *time*

Ⓓ   after *make*

This sentence contains two different ideas, but does not join them with a conjunction. The sentence should read: "We do not have much time; I think we can make it."

EXAMPLE 5

Choose the sentence that shows the correct punctuation.

Ⓐ   We will need shirts, skirts, and dresses for Jane; jackets, lapels, and ties for Miguel; and hats, scarves, and boots for David.

Ⓑ   We will need shirts, skirts, and dresses for Jane, jackets, lapels, and ties for Miguel, and hats, scarves, and boots for David.

Ⓒ   We will need shirts; skirts; and dresses for Jane, jackets; lapels; and ties for Miguel, and hats; scarves; and boots for David.

Ⓓ   We will need shirts, skirts, and dresses for Jane; jackets, lapels, and ties for Miguel, and hats, scarves, and boots for David.

Semicolons are used to separate each person's list, while commas are used to separate the items in each person's list. Choice B is incorrect because it does not use any semicolons, and choice C is incorrect because it uses only semicolons. Choice D is incorrect because the comma after *Miguel* should be a semicolon, separating Miguel's list from David's list.

Colons

A colon (:) is most commonly used to separate hours and minutes when giving the time. For example,

> *5:30 P.M.*
>
> *9:00 A.M.*
>
> *6:45 P.M.*

Colons are also used to introduce a list formally. For example,

> *Here is what Katrina wants for her birthday: a watch, new boots, and a wallet.*

> *We are going to need to do three things to complete this project: research it, construct it, and present it.*

> *There are many professional football teams, including these: the New York Giants, the Indianapolis Colts, and the Chicago Bears.*

EXAMPLE 6

How would you indicate that it was five o'clock in the morning?

Ⓐ   five:00 P.M.

Ⓑ   five:00 A.M.

Ⓒ   5:00 P.M.

Ⓓ   5:00 A.M.

Colons are used to separate numerical hours and minutes when telling time, and *A.M.* indicates morning, while *P.M.* indicates evening.

EXAMPLE 7

Here's what we need to do find him, capture him, and then question him.

Where should you place the colon in this sentence?

Ⓐ   after *what*

Ⓑ   after *do*

Ⓒ   after *we*

Ⓓ   after *need*

Colons can be used to introduce a list. The sentence should read: "Here's what we need to do: find him, capture him, and then question him."

Hyphens and Dashes

Hyphens (-) and dashes (—) are essentially the same type of mark, but they are used differently. A hyphen is a line that is used to join two or more words so that they function as a single word. For example,

> *jump-start*
>
> *hand-fed*
>
> *self-esteem*
>
> *great-grandmother*

A dash, generally typed as a double hyphen, is used

- to emphasize a point. *We went shopping at Donovan's Department Store—where there was a big fire that nearly destroyed the building last year.*
- to mark a break in thought. *His name? It was Mr.—Mr. —hmmm, I can't remember his last name.*
- after an introductory list or series. *Gold, silver, platinum—these are just some of the valuable metals that come from the earth.*

Use the rules of using hyphens and dashes to answer Examples 8 and 9.

EXAMPLE 8

Which of the following words is written correctly?

Ⓐ   double-parked

Ⓑ   ice-cream

Ⓒ   super-market

Ⓓ   land-ing

The two words, *double* and *parked* should be joined to act as a single word. *Ice cream* is a two-word phrase that should not be joined. *Supermarket* is a compound word that should not be separated by a hyphen, and *landing* is a regular word that needs no punctuation of any kind.

EXAMPLE 9

Which sentence uses a dash correctly?

Ⓐ   The girls—were not allowed to dance with boys.

Ⓐ   Milk, eggs, flour—these are common ingredients in most baked goods.

Ⓐ   Don't answer the—phone, because it might be my boss calling.

Ⓓ   Let's go to the theater to—watch a movie.

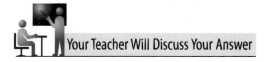
Your Teacher Will Discuss Your Answer

Capitalization

Capital letters, or uppercase letters, are only used in certain circumstances and situations. They are most commonly used at the beginning of a word

- that begins a sentence
- that is a proper name (including people's names and nicknames, geographical names, and the names of languages, organizations, days, months, holidays, historical periods and events, historical documents, and religions)
- that is an abbreviation or acronym (in this case, all letters are usually capitalized)—for example, FBI, YMCA, or NAACP
- that is a personal title preceding the person's name (Dr., Mr., Mrs.)
- that is the first or last word in a title
- that is another important word in a title
- the word *I* (referring to oneself) is also capitalized

EXAMPLE 10

have you met mr. kroger, the owner of qualitec?

Which word or words should be capitalized in this sentence?

Ⓐ have

Ⓑ have, mr., kroger

Ⓒ have, mr., kroger, qualitec

Ⓓ have, mr., kroger, owner, qualitec

The word *have* starts the sentence; *Mr.* is a title that precedes a name; *Kroger* is a proper name; and *Qualitec* is the proper name of an organization. The sentence should be written as follows: "Have you met Mr. Kroger, the owner of Qualitec?"

EXAMPLE 11

Gabriel wrote a book entitled *driving in the moonlight.*

What is the proper way to capitalize the title of this book?

Ⓐ   *Driving in the moonlight*

Ⓑ   *Driving In The Moonlight*

Ⓒ   *Driving in The Moonlight*

Ⓓ   *Driving in the Moonlight*

The first and last word in a title should be capitalized, as should any other important words in the title. Words such as *in, the, an,* and *or* are usually not capitalized, unless they are at the beginning of a title.

EXAMPLE 12

Which of the following words is NOT always capitalized?

Ⓐ   Tuesday

Ⓑ   I

Ⓒ   Jerry

Ⓓ   Often

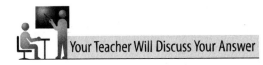
Your Teacher Will Discuss Your Answer

Roots, Prefixes, and Suffixes

A **root** is a basis of a word, to which a prefix or suffix can be added. A **prefix** is something added to the beginning of a word to make a new word. For example, adding <u>un</u>– to the word *deniable*, you can create a new word, *undeniable*. Read through the table below to identify common prefixes and understand how they change a root word.

Common Prefix	Meaning	Example
pre–	before	prehistoric—before recorded history
post–	after	postnatal—after birth
non–	not	nonsense—not sensible
un–	not	unreliable—not reliable
dis–	not	dissatisfied—not satisfied
sub–	under	submarine—under the sea
re–	again	reorder—order again
uni–	single	unidirectional—in one direction
mono–	single	monotone—in a single tone
mis–	wrong	misinformation—wrong information
ex–	out	expel—cast out
inter–	between	interact—actions between two people
anti–	against	anti-smoking—against smoking
pro–	in favor of	pro-war—in favor of war

A **suffix**, like a prefix, is something added to a word to make a new word, but a suffix is added to the end of a word rather than the beginning. For example, adding –<u>less</u> to the word *price* creates the new word, *priceless*. Read through the table below to identify common suffixes and understand how they change a root word.

Suffix	Meaning or Function	Example
–ful	having or being	thoughtful—having thoughts of another
–ive	being	defensive—being in defense of
–less	lacking	tactless—lacking tact
–ly	attributes a quality	quickly—being quick
–ness	state of something	happiness—state of being happy
–able	worthy or capable of	likeable—worthy of being liked
–ible	worthy or capable of	sensible—capable of having sense
–ation	forms nouns from verbs	information—based on verb inform
–ism	act, state, or theory of	heroism—state of being heroic
–ist	one who does something	feminist—one who fights for women
–ology	the study of something	zoology—the study of animals
–ward	in a specific direction	southward—toward the south

EXAMPLE 13

If a person is being unpleasant, you would say that he or she is what?

(A)   subagreeable

(B)   exagreeable

(C)   disagreeable

(D)   reagreeable

By adding the prefix <u>dis</u>– to the word *agreeable*, you create the word *disagreeable*, which means "unpleasant." <u>Sub</u>– refers to something being under something else. <u>Ex</u>– refers to something being out, and <u>re</u>– refers to something being done again.

EXAMPLE 14

Choose the word that is spelled correctly.

(A)   worthles

(B)   inaccurate

(C)   uncarring

(D)   qualifycation

The prefix <u>in</u>– is added to the root *accurate*. Choice A should be spelled *worthless*; choice C should be spelled *uncaring*; and choice D should be spelled *qualification*.

Selection 1

This is a student essay about bubble gum. It contains a number of errors.

Since the days of ancient greece, people have been chewing forms of gum, including *mastiche chicle* and other types of pliable tree sap. A somewhat modern form of chewing gum had been invented and marketed in the united states by a man named Thomas Adams who was trying to find a substitute for rubber in the mid nineteenth century. Actual bubble gum did not come along until the 20th century it was originally invented by Frank Fleer. Fleer's gum, *Blibber-Blubber*, was not very good, and it did not sell.

Bubble gum as we know it today was invented, quite accidentally, in 1928 by a man named Walter Diemer. Mr. Diemer was actually employed as an accountant for the fleer Chewing Gum Company in philadelphia, pennsylvania. In his free time, he enjoyed experimenting with new gum recipes. One day, while concocting a new batch of gum based on Fleer's original recipe, he noticed that what he had was less sticky but more stretchy than normal chewing gum.

As the story goes, he took a five-pound lump of his new gum to a grocery store, and it sold out in a single afternoon! This obviously caught the attention of the Fleer company, his employer, which soon began producing *Dubble Bubble*, selling for a penny a piece. The new chewy treat was pink because it was the only color Mr. Diemer had nearby when creating it. It was very popular, dominating the bubble gum market for years.

In 1930, to increase sales and interest in their product, a comic strip was added under the wrapper of every piece of gum. Each comic featured two characters, Dub and Bub, obviously named for the product. In 1950, Dub and Bub, who had been a *Dubble Bubble* Tradition for twenty years, were replaced by Pud. Pud's adventures are still found in pieces of *Dubble Bubble* today.

As popular as bubble gum was and is, its creator, Mr. Diemer, never patented the recipe and never received any payment for his invention. While this might have upset other people, Mr. Diemer explained that Mr. Deimer was happy to have done something with his life. He once remarked i am just happy to have been able to make so many children all over the world happy.

Go On

1a. **Choose the sentence that does NOT contain a modifier.**

Ⓐ   It was very popular.

Ⓑ   This obviously caught the attention of the Fleer company, his employer.

Ⓒ   Fleer's gum, *Blibber-Blubber*, was not very good, and it did not sell.

Ⓓ   A somewhat modern form of chewing gum had been invented and marketed in the united states by a man named Thomas Adams.

1b. **Which of the following sentences is written in the active voice?**

Ⓐ   Pud's adventures are still found in pieces of *Dubble Bubble* today.

Ⓑ   He took a five-pound lump of his new gum to a grocery store, and it sold out in a single afternoon!

Ⓒ   A somewhat modern form of chewing gum had been invented and marketed in the united states by a man named Thomas Adams.

Ⓓ   A comic strip was added under the wrapper of every piece of gum.

1c. **Which sentence from this essay contains an infinitive?**

Ⓐ   He took a five-pound lump of his new gum to a grocery store, and it sold out in a single afternoon!

Ⓑ   As popular as bubble gum was and is, its creator, Mr. Diemer, never patented the recipe.

Ⓒ   In 1930, to increase sales and interest in their product, a comic strip was added under the wrapper of every piece of gum.

Ⓓ   Each comic featured two characters, Dub and Bub, obviously named for the product.

Go On

Written English Language Applications

1d. **Choose the sentence that contains a participle used as an adjective.**

    Ⓐ   It was very popular, dominating the bubble gum market for years.

    Ⓑ   A comic strip was added under the wrapper of every piece of gum.

    Ⓒ   As popular as bubble gum was and is, its creator, Mr. Diemer, never patented the recipe.

    Ⓓ   Pud's adventures are still found in pieces of Dubble Bubble today.

1e. **Choose the BEST way to rewrite this sentence.**

Mr. Diemer explained that Mr. Deimer was happy to have done something with his life.

    Ⓐ   Mr. Diemer explained that they were happy to have done something with his life.

    Ⓑ   Mr. Diemer explained that she was happy to have done something with his life.

    Ⓒ   Mr. Diemer explained that him were happy to have done something with his life.

    Ⓓ   Mr. Diemer explained that he was happy to have done something with his life.

Go On

1f. **Choose the BEST way to rewrite this sentence.**

Actual bubble gum did not come along until the 20th century it was originally invented by Frank Fleer.

Ⓐ Actual bubble gum did not come along until the 20th century; it was originally invented by Frank Fleer.

Ⓑ Actual bubble gum did not come along until the 20th century: it was originally invented by Frank Fleer.

Ⓒ "Actual bubble gum did not come along until the 20th century it was originally invented by Frank Fleer."

Ⓓ Actual bubble gum did not come along, until the 20th century, it was originally invented by Frank Fleer.

1g. **Rewrite this sentence using proper punctuation and capitalization.**

He once remarked i am just happy to have been able to make so many children all over the world happy.

_____

_____

_____

Go On

1h. Which word or words in this sentence should be capitalized but are not?

Mr. Diemer was actually employed as an accountant for the fleer Chewing Gum Company in philadelphia, pennsylvania.

Ⓐ   accountant

Ⓑ   accountant, fleer

Ⓒ   philadelphia, pennsylvania, and accountant

Ⓓ   philadelphia, pennsylvania, fleer

1i. Which word in this sentence should NOT be capitalized?

In 1950, Dub and Bub, who had been a Dubble Bubble Tradition for twenty years, were replaced by Pud.

Ⓐ   Tradition

Ⓑ   Pud

Ⓒ   Dubble

Ⓓ   Bubble

Go On

1j. The first attempts at bubble gum were not very good. Another way to say this would be to say that the first attempts at bubble gum produced substances that were

- Ⓐ   deeatable

- Ⓑ   inedible

- Ⓒ   prochewable

- Ⓓ   tastyless

1k. Rewrite this sentence correctly, using proper punctuation and capitalization.

Since the days of ancient greece, people have been chewing forms of gum, including *mastiche chicle* and other types of pliable tree sap.

_____

_____

_____

_____

1l. Rewrite this sentence correctly, using proper punctuation and capitalization.

A somewhat modern form of chewing gum had been invented and marketed in the united states by a man named Thomas Adams, who was trying to find a substitute for rubber, in the mid nineteenth century.

_____

_____

_____

_____

STOP

Written English Language Applications

Unit 5

The Writing Process

The Indiana Indicators addressed in this unit include:

7.4.1 Students should be able to discuss ideas for writing, keep a list or notebook of ideas, and use graphic organizers to plan writing.

7.4.2 Students should be able to create an organizational structure that balances all aspects of the composition and uses effective transitions between sentences to unify important ideas.

7.4.3 Students should understand how to support all statements and claims with anecdotes, descriptions, facts and statistics, and specific examples.

7.4.4 Students should be able to use strategies of note-taking, outlining, and summarizing to impose structure on composition drafts.

7.4.5 Students should understand how to identify topics; ask and evaluate questions; and develop ideas leading to inquiry, investigation, and research.

7.4.6 Students should understand how to give credit for both quoted and paraphrased information in a bibliography by using a consistent format for citations.

7.4.8 Students should be able to review, evaluate, and revise writing for meaning and clarity.

7.4.9 Students should be able to proofread their own writing, as well as that of others, using an editing checklist or set of rules, with specific examples of corrections of frequent errors.

7.4.10 Students should understand how to revise writing to improve organization and word choice after checking the logic of the ideas and the precision of the vocabulary.

GETTING the IDEA

In order to write effectively, you need to know how to identify topics for writing and take notes; use outlines and graphic organizers to map out your writing; develop supporting statements and include details that provide evidence in support of your argument; use transitions to move from paragraph to paragraph; and prepare and organize sentences to make an effective argument. You will also need to know how to prepare and include reference notations, including endnotes and bibliographic references.

Before preparing your first draft, you will need to determine exactly what it is you will be writing about, and then you must research your topic and take notes. After you have your notes, you will need to prepare an outline and a graphic organizer which will lay out the order in which you will present your information, as well as identify the specific types of information you will include. In your writing, you will need to identify the sources of information for the claims you have made.

After you have completed your first draft, you will need to go through what you have written and make corrections. This unit explains how to go about reviewing, evaluating, proofreading, editing, and revising your work to make your presentation as clear and understandable as possible. It also discusses the importance of using a variety of words when you write, to make your writing more interesting and accurate.

Chapter 7

Organizing and Focusing Research

Identifying Topics

As you perform your research, you will come across far more information than necessary to complete your paper. What you will need to do, then, is to identify a specific topic on which to focus your writing.

The first step toward identifying your topic is asking questions. Ask yourself what kind of information you are looking for, what kind of information you are uncovering, and what you can do with the information you find.

Next, you should evaluate your answers. Think about the kind of information you are coming across. Does it seem too advanced or specific for your purposes? Is it too general? Is there enough information available for you to write an adequate paper? Is there too much information to cover in a single essay? Is the information reliable and factual, or theoretical and questionable?

These questions, answers, and evaluations will help direct your research and will aid you in determining your final topic and the approach you will take to it. This technique is closely related to the process of asking framing questions, which you will learn more about in Chapter 11.

EXAMPLE 1

Your teacher has assigned you to write a one-page essay about a former U.S. president. Which of the following questions should you ask yourself FIRST when you start your research?

Ⓐ   How many U.S. presidents have there been?

Ⓑ   Who are the former U.S. presidents?

Ⓒ   Which president Roosevelt led the country during World War II?

Ⓓ   What are the requirements for becoming president?

Before you can delve too deeply into this assignment, you would first need to identify the list of potential subjects for your paper. Choice A is incorrect because it is the names of the former presidents that is important, not the number of them. Choice C is incorrect because this is a question you would probably not ask until later in the research stage. Choice D is incorrect because it does not directly relate to the assignment.

EXAMPLE 2

Let's say that you have decided to make President James K. Polk the subject of your paper. Which of the following questions should you ask yourself next?

Ⓐ   When was Polk the president?

Ⓑ   Who was president before Polk?

Ⓒ   Was Polk voted out of office, or did he choose not to run again?

Ⓓ   Should I focus on the life of Polk or only his achievements in office?

 Your Teacher Will Discuss Your Answer

Note-Taking and Outlining

Before you begin writing, you will need to compile information about the topic you will be writing about. Once you have located sources from which to take the information, you will need to take notes. Review the list below for suggestions for effective note-taking.

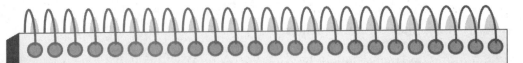

Note-Taking Strategies

- Know what kind of information you are looking for. While you might come across some interesting information, if it is not relevant to your assignment, it is likely useless to you.

- Make a preliminary list of the subtopics you expect to find information about.

- Take down the most relevant information.

- Focus on facts and avoid opinions.

- Do not waste time writing every word. You can omit simple words such as *the* and *an* when you know you will not be confused by their absence.

- Use your own words as much as possible when taking notes. This will help you to clarify your thinking and avoid the possibility of plagiarism.

- Use a separate page or note card for each different source, so you can later identify where you located the information.

- Take down all the information about the source you are using, so that you will be able to format endnotes and a bibliography without having to locate the source again.

- Leave blank spaces between points. This allows you to quickly locate and identify information, and also provides room to add another point you might come across.

- Leave enough room in the margins for your own additional notes.

- Write large enough and neatly enough so that you will have no difficulty reading your own notes later.

- When taking notes, follow a uniform pattern as much as possible. For example, your notes might follow the sequence of events involved in what you are researching.

EXAMPLE 3

Which of the following would you want to do when taking notes?

Ⓐ   Modify your note-taking style for each resource you use.

Ⓑ   Fill the paper completely, from edge to edge, leaving no spaces.

Ⓒ   Use your own words.

Ⓓ   Write down every word from the resource you are using.

When taking notes, using your own words helps you to better understand what you are writing. It helps you to avoid unintentionally plagiarizing copyrighted material, or presenting someone else's words as your own.

EXAMPLE 4

When taking notes for a paper, you should NOT

Ⓐ   focus on opinions

Ⓑ   use different pages or note cards for different sources

Ⓒ   leave room in the margins

Ⓓ   write legibly

You should focus on facts rather than opinions, because your paper should be based in fact. You can add your own opinion, if appropriate, in the paper.

After you have taken notes, you will need to develop an outline to organize the information you have found. The outline will act as the "map" of your paper, identifying the main topics you will discuss, subtopics or supporting evidence for main topics, and the order in which you will present them.

To set up your outline, determine the major points and topics that you will discuss, and then organize them in the order in which you want to present them, marking them with upper-case Roman numerals. You should also include the introduction and conclusion in your outline. For example, let's say you're writing a paper about beagles. Your primary topics might include:

      I. **Introduction**

     II. **General Appearance**

   III. **Characteristics**

   IV. **Temperament**

    V. **Conclusion**

Next, you should add subtopics for each topic, marking these with capital letters and indenting beneath the primary topic:

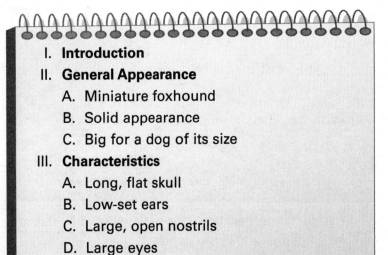

      I. **Introduction**
     II. **General Appearance**
         A. Miniature foxhound
         B. Solid appearance
         C. Big for a dog of its size
   III. **Characteristics**
         A. Long, flat skull
         B. Low-set ears
         C. Large, open nostrils
         D. Large eyes
   IV. **Temperament**
         A. Friendly
         B. Can easily be trained to obey commands
    V. **Conclusion**

You can continue to lay out additional points by following the same pattern. Just indent beneath the point you want to clarify further, and introduce a different type of numbering or lettering. For example:

I. **Introduction**
II. **General Appearance**
   A. Miniature foxhound
   B. Solid appearance
   C. Big for a dog of its size
      1. Tends to be heavy
      2. Eats a lot of food daily
III. **Characteristics**
   A. Long, flat skull
   B. Low-set ears
   C. Large, open nostrils
   D. Large eyes
IV. **Temperament**
   A. Friendly
   B. Can easily be trained to obey commands
      1. Can be taught to heel and stay
      2. Discourage cringing and sulking
V. **Conclusion**

EXAMPLE 5

Which of the following should always be the first main heading in an outline for a research paper?

Ⓐ   framing question

Ⓑ   introduction

Ⓒ   supporting statement

Ⓓ   conclusion

The outline is a "map" of your paper, or the "route" you will take when writing. The first part of any paper is the introduction and should be the first item on your outline.

EXAMPLE 6

The first level of numbering on an outline should use which type of symbols?

Ⓐ   capital letters

Ⓑ   lower-case letters

Ⓒ   Roman numerals

Ⓓ   standard numerals

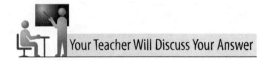

Using Graphic Organizers

Before you start to write, you should know what you are going to write about. To do this, you should think about your topic, and then organize your ideas.

One way to organize your ideas is through the use of a **graphic organizer**. A graphic organizer is a tool you can use to illustrate your ideas visually. Your primary topic goes in the main box, while related ideas and topics "branch out" into other boxes. For example, the graphic organizer below might be used by a person writing a report about the effects of acid rain.

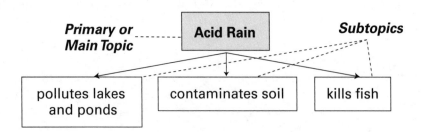

In this example, the main topic is acid rain, and the secondary topics involve how acid rain pollutes bodies of water, kills fish, and contaminates soil. Additional subtopics could branch off the main topic, and sub-subtopics could also branch off from any of the subtopics. For example, if you were going to write a paper about Bill Clinton, the graphic organizer might look something like this:

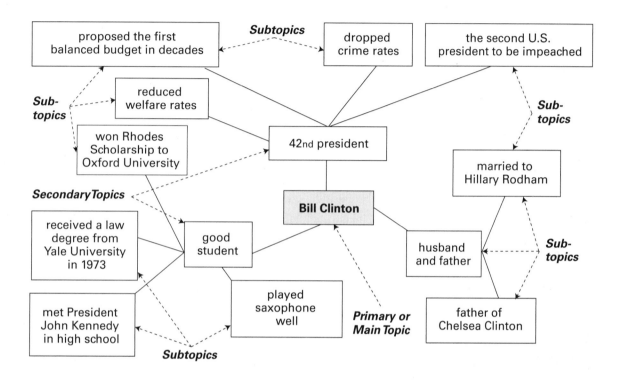

It is also important to note that graphic organizers can take a variety of forms. In addition to the two styles shown above, the sequential flowchart style is also common. This is often used when organizing information or events into sequential order.

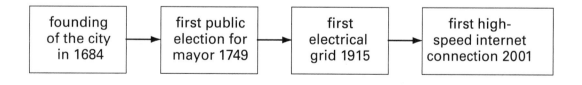

EXAMPLE 7

Which box contains the primary writing topic?

Ⓐ A

Ⓑ B

Ⓒ C

Ⓓ D

The primary topic is the one topic that all other topics relate to. In this case, the primary topic of the paper is the telephone, with the three subtopics involving its invention, evolution, and modern innovations.

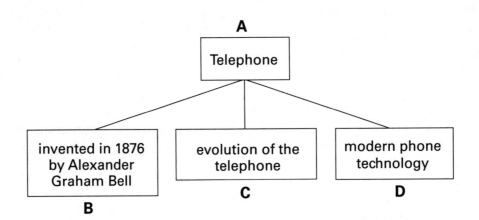

126

Supporting Statements

When making claims or statements in a paper, you should provide supporting information to illustrate, verify, or enhance the point. Methods of supporting statements include the use of

- anecdotes
- descriptions
- facts and statistics
- specific examples

Anecdotes

An anecdote is a short, first-person account of something. When appropriate, a claim may be backed up by a brief story that illustrates the point made by the claim. For example, if you made the claim that there are many fun things to do at summer camp, you would want to follow up with a quick story about fun things you have done at camp. By adding an anecdote after a claim, you can provide evidence that supports your claim and makes your paper more interesting for your reader at the same time.

Descriptions

Descriptions can be used to enhance a claim by providing more details about what you are writing about. For example, if you claimed that cougars are frightening creatures, you would want to add a description of the animal, writing about its long teeth, strong body, speed, and violent nature. When writing, you should use descriptions to help the reader "see" what you are talking about and to direct the mental images he or she has while reading.

Facts and Statistics

Facts and statistics are some of the best types of supporting evidence, because their validity generally cannot be questioned. They can be used to provide specific information in support of a general claim. For example, if you wrote that the crime rate in the city had dropped in the last year, you could follow that statement up with official crime statistics and facts, such as "There were 50% fewer murders and 20% fewer assaults in 2003 than in 2002." By including facts and statistics, your argument will seem more valid, and the reader will be more confident that you know what you are stating.

Specific Examples

Examples are useful tools for helping to illustrate a point you are trying to make. For example, the statement "Snakes can be dangerous" is broad, and it leaves it up to the reader to determine how dangerous snakes can be. However, if you add examples, you can clarify your meaning.

> *Snakes can be dangerous creatures. For example, the venom of the Australian Brown Snake is so potent that 1/14,000th of an ounce is enough to kill a person. The bite of a Taipan delivers enough venom to kill up to 12,000 guinea pigs.*

When you provide a specific example, it makes it easier for the reader to understand the point you are trying to make.

EXAMPLE 8

In a paper you are writing, you make the claim that a well being dug by geologists in the Kola Peninsula in Russia is the deepest man-made hole in the world. Which of the following would be the BEST supporting evidence to back up this claim?

Ⓐ   an anecdote about well-digging

Ⓑ   a description of the equipment used to dig the hole

Ⓒ   statistics identifying the depth of other very deep man-made holes

Ⓓ   an example of a type of rock found in the hole

If you are claiming that this is the deepest man-made hole on Earth, you would want to compare it to other deep man-made holes. The best way to do this would be to provide facts and statistics about the most comparable man-made holes.

Using Details and Transitions

An important key to effective writing is ensuring that your paragraphs flow logically from one to the next. The best way to do this is to use appropriate details and transitions when writing.

Details can be used to link paragraphs when one or more details from one paragraph are reflected in, or otherwise related to, details in the next paragraph. For example:

> *The leek is a relative of garlic and the onion. It has a more mild and subtle flavor than its relatives. It can be cooked whole or diced and used as a salad or soup topping.*
>
> *Shallots, on the other hand, more closely resemble garlic than onion. They have a head of multiple cloves, each covered with a thin, paper-like skin. They can be used as a substitute for onions in most recipes.*

Details from the first paragraph, including the relation to garlic and onion, are seen again in the second paragraph. Presenting information this way allows the writer to provide new information in an easy-to-grasp, flowing manner. Readers can be distracted or confused by paragraphs that transition awkwardly. Mirroring details can help you to avoid that problem.

Another effective way of linking paragraphs is through the use of transitions. **Transitions** are movements from one topic to another that use words and phrases which state or imply relationships. Examples of transitional words and phrases can be seen in the table below.

Type of transition	Examples
addition	again, also, as well, besides, furthermore, in addition, moreover
consequence	accordingly, as a result, consequently, hence, otherwise, so then, therefore, thus
contrast/ comparison	but, by the same token, conversely, however, instead, likewise, nevertheless, on one hand, on the other hand, on the contrary, rather, similarly, still, yet
diversion	by the way, incidentally
direction	above, below, beyond, here, in the distance, nearly, opposite, over there, over here, there, to the left, to the right
generalizing	as a rule, as usual, for the most part, generally, generally speaking, ordinarily, usually
illustration	for example, for instance, for one thing, for another thing
sequence	afterward, at first, at the same time, first of all, for now, for the time being, earlier, later, while, next, later on, meanwhile, in the first place, simultaneously, in conclusion
similarity	likewise, similarly, moreover
summarizing	after all, all in all, all things considered, briefly, by and large, finally, in any case, in any event, in brief, in conclusion, on the whole, in short, in summary, in the long run, to sum up, to summarize

EXAMPLE 9

Blaize is a runner. He gets up early every morning and jogs the circumference of the pond at Parker's Manner. He loves to run marathons recreationally and practices for them for months beforehand.

One marathon training technique that Blaize can be seen practicing on weekends is the long, slow distance run. He runs for two and a half hours alternating his pace between walking, jogging, and running backwards.

What transitional tool is used to link these two paragraphs?

Ⓐ   details

Ⓑ   summarizing transitional word/phrases

Ⓒ   sequential transitional words/phrases

Ⓓ   directional transitional words/phrases

Details from the first paragraph, including running and marathon training, are seen again in the second paragraph.

EXAMPLE 10

The first step in making a pizza is finding the right dough. It is important that you use pizza dough rather than bread dough. The two types of dough are made slightly differently, because they serve different purposes. Pizza dough is not intended to rise as much as bread dough, and bread dough is not intended to be spread as thin as pizza dough.

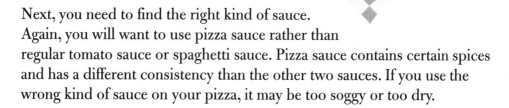

Next, you need to find the right kind of sauce. Again, you will want to use pizza sauce rather than regular tomato sauce or spaghetti sauce. Pizza sauce contains certain spices and has a different consistency than the other two sauces. If you use the wrong kind of sauce on your pizza, it may be too soggy or too dry.

What type of transitional word or phrase is used to link these two passages?

Ⓐ   illustration

Ⓑ   sequence

Ⓒ   direction

Ⓓ   diversion

The paragraphs each start with a sequential transitional word, in this case *first* and *next*, which indicates when each step should take place.

Sentences

Just as a paper should have introductory and concluding paragraphs, individual paragraphs should have introductory and concluding sentences. The introductory sentence of a paragraph is known as the **topic sentence**. A topic sentence is the sentence that establishes the topic of the paragraph. While it is often the first sentence in a paragraph, the topic sentence may actually be found almost anywhere in the paragraph. It is also the sentence to which all other sentences in the paragraph relate. For example,

> *The people that benefit from public services are the members of the public. Anyone who has been robbed can call the police. Any time there is a fire, the fire department can be called to come put it out. Any child in this country can receive a free public education. In private business, though, the only people that benefit from the goods or services purchased are those that purchase them. A private security guard hired by a company to guard its plant will not try to find the person that broke into your house. Only those children whose families paid tuition can attend private schools. Public services are more extensive than private services.*

In this paragraph, the opening statement is the topic sentence: *The people that benefit from public services are the members of the public.* All of the other sentences in this paragraph are related to that sentence, either by illustrating examples of ways that members of the public benefit, or by explaining how private services are not beneficial to all members of the public.

A **concluding sentence** is a sentence that ends a paragraph. A concluding sentence may summarize the argument of a paragraph, restate a point made in the topic sentence, or otherwise draw the paragraph to a close. In the example above, the concluding sentence is "Public Services are more extensive than private services." This sentence summarizes the main ideas presented in the paragraph by pointing to a logical connection between them.

EXAMPLE 11

Which of the following is a characteristic of a topic sentence?

Ⓐ   All other sentences relate directly to it.

Ⓑ   None of the other sentences relate directly to it.

Ⓒ   It is always the first sentence in the paragraph.

Ⓓ   It is always the last sentence in the paragraph.

Because the topic sentence establishes the topic for the paragraph, every other sentence in the paragraph relates to it. While it is often the first sentence in the paragraph, it can also be the second, third, fourth, etc.

EXAMPLE 12

The concluding sentence

Ⓐ   ends the paragraph

Ⓑ   may restate the argument of the topic sentence

Ⓒ   both A and B

Ⓓ   neither A nor B

 Your Teacher Will Discuss Your Answer

Writing Sentences in Order

Just as you want to present the paragraphs in a paper in order, you want to do the same with sentences in a paragraph. Generally, you should open with a topic sentence, follow with supporting sentences, and then end with a concluding sentence. The topic sentence presents the argument or subject of discussion for the paragraph. The supporting sentences provide more information about the topic sentence or illustrate the point made in the topic sentence. The concluding sentence ends the paragraph. For example, consider which would be the BEST way to organize these sentences.

1. *They live in trees and eat eucalyptus leaves.*

2. *Koalas get 90% of their hydration from the liquid in the leaves.*

3. *The word* koala *comes from the aboriginal language, and means "no drink".*

4. *Koalas are small bear-like creatures that live in Australia.*

5. *They generally drink only when the leaves are dry, such as during droughts.*

The first sentence in the paragraph should be the topic sentence. In this case, that would be sentence 4. The next sentence should build upon the topic sentence in some way. In this case, it should provide further description of koala bears. The most logical second sentence, then, would be sentence 1. So far, the paragraph should look like this:

> *Koalas are small bear-like creatures that live in Australia. They live in trees and eat eucalyptus leaves.*

The remainder of the sentences should follow the same pattern, building on the sentence that immediately comes before it. In this example, the next sentence would be 3, followed by sentences 2 and 5.

> *Koalas are small bear-like creatures that live in Australia. They live in trees and eat eucalyptus leaves. The word* koala *comes from the aboriginal language, and means "no drink". Koalas get 90% of their hydration from the liquid in the leaves. They generally drink only when the leaves are dry, such as during droughts.*

Sentence 3, which talks about the meaning of the word *koala*, further builds on the general topic of koalas, and sentences 2 and 5, which talk about how the koala receives hydration, build upon sentence 3.

The important thing to remember in sentence ordering is to present your sentences in a logical order that the reader will be able to understand easily.

EXAMPLE 13

Choose the BEST way to order these sentences in a paragraph.

1. Mid-level clouds are found between 6,500 and 23,000 feet, and are made up of liquid water droplets in the summer and a droplet-ice crystal mix in the winter.

2. One way in which clouds can be categorized is by their location, or level above the earth.

3. High-level clouds are found above 23,000 feet and are made up of ice crystals because water freezes quickly at that altitude.

4. Low-level clouds are found below 6,500 feet and are made up of liquid water droplets.

Ⓐ   1, 2, 3, 4

Ⓑ   2, 1, 3, 4

Ⓒ   2, 4, 1, 3

Ⓓ   4, 3, 2, 1

Sentence 2 is the topic sentence, which introduces the paragraph. The rest of the sentences should follow in a logical manner. In this case, you would want to organize the sentences in the order of cloud levels discussed. Start with low-level clouds, follow with mid-level clouds, and conclude with high-level clouds.

Using Organizational Features: Endnotes and Bibliographic References

Most of the time when you write a report, you first need to research the topic you are writing about. When you use information you found in source such as an encyclopedia or magazine article, you need to make a notation in your paper indicating the source of your information. The two most common tools for making such notations are endnotes and bibliographic references.

Endnotes

Endnotes are a list of sources used in researching a paper, found at the end of the report. Each reference made in the body of the paper to an outside source must be documented in an endnote.

When making a reference to a source in the body of the paper , you should provide a number which will correspond with the numbered endnote. The number should be slightly raised in comparison to the other text, so that the reader knows that it is intended as a citation. For example,

> During the Civil War, 5,867,000 Americans lost their lives.[5]

This notation indicates that the source of this information can be found in endnote number 5.

The format of endnotes is standardized, so you should not try to personalize the way you do your endnotes. The basic format for different types of endnotes are as follows.

Book by a single author

Endnote number Author's name, Book Title (publication location: publisher name, publication date) page number.

Example:

> [1] Maddy Klein, Peace and Calm (Los Angeles: Bluebird Press, 1992) 80.

Book by multiple authors

Endnote number Author one and Author two, <u>Book Title</u> (publication location: publisher name, publication date) page number.

Example:

> [2] Bryant James and Sandra Schulz, <u>Abraham Lincoln</u> (Seattle: Morningside Publishers, 1980) 128.

If there are more than two authors, use commas to separate their names.

Encyclopedia Entry

Endnote number Author's name or Editor's name, Book Title, volume number (publication location: publisher name, publication date) page number.

Examples:

> [3] Brianne McCourt, <u>Heritage Encyclopedia</u>, vol. 8 (Chicago: Sun Press, 1976) 42.

> [3] "Louis Armstrong", <u>Encyclopedia of Music</u>, 1976 ed.

Newspaper Article

Endnote number Author's name, "Article Title," <u>Newspaper Name</u> publication date publication month publication year, edition, section: page number.

Example:

> [4] Sam Ash, "Hendrix Revisited," <u>Nashville Tribune</u> 24 May 1990, final ed., sec. 4: 2.

Magazine Article

Endnote number Author's name, "Article Title," <u>Magazine Name</u> publication date publication month publication year: page number.

Example:

> [5] Stephanie Law, "Dealing with Divorce," <u>Time In</u> 15 Mar. 2004: 23.

EXAMPLE 14

Choose the correct way to format an endnote for an article called "Globalization" found on page 64 in volume 6 of the 2002 edition of the *Heritage Encyclopedia*, published by Sun Press, located in Chicago. The name of the editor is Norma Perez.

Ⓐ   [3] Norma Perez, "Globalization" Heritage Encyclopedia 2002: 64.

Ⓑ   [3] Norma Perez, Heritage Encyclopedia, vol.6 (Chicago: Sun Press, 2002) 64.

Ⓒ   [3] Norma Perez, Heritage Encyclopedia (Chicago: Sun Press, 2002) 64.

Ⓓ   [3] Norma Perez, "Globalization" Heritage Encyclopedia 2002, final ed., sec 1: 64.

Choice B is the only option that follows the standardized encyclopedia notation format.

Bibliographic References

A **bibliography** is the list of resources used in researching a paper. Unlike endnotes, which cite specific pages where specific information was found, the bibliography lists all of the books, magazines, and other sources used.

Like endnotes, a bibliography uses a standardized format that must always be followed. The bibliographic references are not numbered to match up with citations within the body of the work. Instead, they are organized alphabetically by the first letter in the first major word in each citation. The basic format for different types of publications is as follows.

Book with One Author

Author's last name, Author's first name. Book Title. City of publication: Publisher, Publication date.

Example:

Culbert, Jill. Ethics and Law. San Diego: Earth Press, 2000.

Book with Multiple Authors

Author names should be given in the same order they are given in the book.

First Author's last name, first author's first name, and second Author's last name, second Author's first name. <u>Book Title</u>. City of publication: publisher, publication date.

Example:

>Lonial, Deepak, and Brown, Jane. <u>Breaking the Code</u>. New York: Splash Publications, 1984.

Encyclopedia

If the author's name is not available, use the editor's name. If neither is available, begin with the title of the article.

Author's last name, Author's first name. "Article Title." <u>Publication Title</u>. Date of edition.

Example:

>Bello, Nicole. "Acid Rain." <u>Scholastic Encyclopedia</u>. 1994.

Periodical Article (Magazine or Newspaper)

Author's last name, Author's first name. "Article Title." <u>Periodical Title</u> date month year: page.

Example:

>Rainone, Andy. "Peace in the Middle East." <u>New York Light</u> 18 Dec. 1999: B6.

EXAMPLE 15

Choose the correct way to note a bibliographic entry for a book titled <u>Culture Clash</u>, written by David Pace and published by Academic Press of St. Louis in 1998.

Ⓐ   David Pace. "Culture Clash" St. Louis: Academic Press, 1998.

Ⓑ   Pace, David. "Culture Clash" St. Louis: Academic Press, 1998.

Ⓒ   Pace, David. <u>Culture Clash</u>. St. Louis: Academic Press, 1998.

Ⓓ   David Pace. <u>Culture Clash</u>. St. Louis: Academic Press, 1998.

The only option that follows the standardized format for a bibliographic reference for a book by a single author is choice C.

Unit 5

Writing Practice

Read the writing prompt below, and complete the writing activity.

My Favorite Season

In many parts of the world, the weather does not change much from season to season. It's always relatively cold in the Arctic Circle, and it's always relatively hot and rainy around the Equator. In most of the United States, though, we experience four seasons: spring, summer, autumn, and winter. Everybody seems to like different seasons for different reasons. What is your favorite season of the year?

Write an essay in which you identify your favorite season of the year, and give TWO reasons why that particular season is your favorite.

Be sure to include

- the name of your favorite season
- two reasons why that season is your favorite
- explanations that support your reasons
- details and/or transitions that smoothly shift the essay from paragraph to paragraph
- an introduction, body, and a conclusion to your essay

_____

_____

_____

_____

_____

Go On

_____

_____

_____

_____

_____

_____

_____

_____

_____

_____

_____

_____

_____

_____

_____

_____

_____

_____

_____

_____

Chapter 8

Reviewing, Evaluating, and Revising

Nobody is perfect, especially when it comes to writing. Generally speaking, when you write, you are not writing a final draft right away. When you first attempt to write a paper, your primary goal is to provide the information you want to provide and say what you want to say. Because you are focusing on getting the information in writing, you are likely to make errors in spelling, grammar, and punctuation. It is also common for a first draft to include errors in clarity, meaning that what you have written is not exactly what you intended to say. After you have finished your first draft you need to review, evaluate, and revise it.

Reviewing

Reviewing your writing means going back to the beginning and reading what you have written. When reviewing, be sure to read slowly and pay attention to the words on the page. It is very easy to miss a mistake when you try to read too quickly. When reviewing, look for:

- misspelled words
- errors in grammar, such as the wrong verb tense, misplaced modifiers, etc.
- inconsistency—This means that you should review the content to make sure that what you have written actually makes sense as it is written.
- confusing words or statements—You want your writing to be as clear and understandable as possible. If something you have written does not make sense to you, it probably will not make sense to the person reading your paper.

Most importantly, you want to be sure that what you have written matches what you are supposed to be writing about. A well-written paper that does not contain the information the teacher is looking for will result in a poor grade.

Reviewing Strategies

- Read your writing out loud. If something does not sound right, it probably is not right.
- Read silently in reverse. Start with the last word on the page and read backward. This can help you to identify errors in spelling that you might have missed during your initial read-through.
- When possible, have someone else review what you have written *after* you have reviewed it yourself. Do not rely on someone else to catch all of your mistakes.

Evaluating

Evaluating refers to making determinations about what you have written. When you review your work, ask yourself these questions:

- Does this sentence/paragraph make sense?
- Have I spelled any words incorrectly?
- Have I used proper sentence structure? (Are there any sentence fragments? Do nouns and verbs agree? Is my grammar appropriate?)
- Does the content of the paper match the assignment?
- Is my writing clear and to the point?

When evaluating your writing, make notes on your paper about things you want to change. Circle misspelled words or improperly structured sentences, and make notes in the margins about other changes.

Revising

After you have reviewed and evaluated your writing, you can begin revising. This means that you will rewrite the paper (or edit it on the computer if it was typed), making any necessary changes. Pay close attention to your writing during the revising stage. When you revise, you want your paper to be as perfect as you can make it.

Proofreading: Using an Editing Checklist

Proofreading is the process of reading your writing and looking for errors in grammar, spelling, and structure. When it is time to proofread your work, use the editing checklist below to identify potential problems with your writing.

> ## *Editing Checklist*
>
> **1** Check your capitalization and punctuation.
>
> **2** Spell all words correctly.
>
> **3** Check for sentence fragments or run-on sentences.
>
> **4** Keep verb tense consistent.
>
> **5** Make sure subject and verb agree.
>
> **6** Use words according to the rules of Standard English.
>
> **7** Remember to paragraph correctly.

EXAMPLE 1

This is a sample passage from a student essay about federalism. It contains a number of errors.

(1) Federalism is the sharing of power between the states and the national (federal) government. (2) The u.s. government was organized to provide a central government that serves basic purposes of national interest, such as providing national security and establishing basic universal rights. (3) The majority of power was intended to be held by the individual states, following the model of the federal government but creates, enforces, and interprets their own laws. (4) This approach to governmint protects individual rights. (5) It allow the people of a particular region, specifically in a state, to set their own rules and standards, giving them more control over their own government. (6) It also protects the common good. (7) By ensuring this same opportunity to all members of the public. (8) Checks and balances are another tool for maintaining the balance of power in government. (9) This system allows each branch of the government to have some influence over the other branches.

Which of the following sentences does NOT contain any errors?

Ⓐ   1

Ⓑ   3

Ⓒ   4

Ⓓ   5

Of these choices, only sentence 1 does not contain any errors. In sentence 3, "creates, enforces, and interprets" should be "creating, enforcing, and interpreting." In sentence 4, the word *governmint* should be spelled *government*. The subject and verb in sentence 5 do not agree, so the word *allow* must be changed to *allows*.

EXAMPLE 2

Referring to the same passage, choose the sentence that is actually a sentence fragment.

Ⓐ   2

Ⓑ   4

Ⓒ   7

Ⓓ   9

Sentence 7 does not contain a main clause. It could act as a phrase in a complete sentence, though. For example, it could be combined with sentence 6 to read, "It also protects the common good by ensuring this same opportunity to all members of the public." Each of the other three sentences has a main clause, so each can be considered a complete sentence.

EXAMPLE 3

Referring to the same passage again, choose where you should start a new paragraph.

Ⓐ   after sentence 2

Ⓑ   after sentence 6

Ⓒ   after sentence 7

Ⓓ   after sentence 8

You should begin a new paragraph after sentence 7, meaning that sentence 8 would be the topic sentence of the next paragraph. This is the most logical place to split the paragraph because that sentence begins a new topic, checks and balances.

Editing and Revising

Editing is the process of preparing your paper for its final draft. Editing differs from proofreading in that proofreading focuses on spelling and grammar errors, while editing focuses on content problems. This means that when you edit, you change the way in which you present information to help ensure clarity. This may involve:

- adding and deleting sentences
- combining sentences
- rearranging words and sentences

Adding and Deleting Sentences

Good writing is clear, concise, and focused. This means that when you write, you should be sure that each paragraph contains only the information relevant to the topic. This often involves adding and deleting sentences.

When you are reading through your work, you might come across a section where you realize you have more to say in a particular section. Maybe there is an additional point you want to make, or maybe you want to further justify or describe something. When you have more to say, you will want to add a sentence or several sentences. When you do this, be sure to read the paragraph completely to identify where you need to add more sentences. Then write the new sentence or sentences, and insert them where you feel they make the most sense. If you are working on paper, write the sentence in the margin (or other available space near the paragraph) and then draw an arrow indicating where the sentence should be inserted into the paragraph. If you are working on a computer, you can merely type the sentence wherever you feel it should go. When you are done, re-read the paragraph to be sure that the new paragraph reads exactly the way that you want it to.

A relevant sentence fits the context of the paragraph and makes sense in relation to the other sentences. An irrelevant sentence may or may not relate to another sentence in the paragraph, but it does not fit in with the paragraph as a whole. Sometimes when reading through your own work, you come across sentences that are repetitive, seem out of place, or are completely unnecessary. Such sentences are irrelevant and should be deleted. If you are working on paper, simply draw a line through the sentence so you know not to copy it when you rewrite the page. If you are working on a computer, you can delete the sentence using the "backspace" or "delete" key. Just as with adding sentences, after you have deleted sentences, re-read the paragraph to be sure that it now says what you want it to say.

EXAMPLE 4

Read the following passage, and then answer the questions that follow.

(1) Many colors have been linked to human emotions, a connection which is reflected in our use of language. (2) Red, for example, is often associated with feelings of anger or passion, such as in the phrase "red with anger." (3) Blue is connected with feelings of sadness and melancholy, as reflected in the genre of music known as the blues, which is characterized by sad, depressing songs. (4) I sometimes feel sad in the winter, when the days are so short. (5) Yellow indicates fear, such as in the term "yellowbelly," and most of us have heard a person referred to as "green with envy" at some point in our lives. (6) As you study the English language, you will likely be able to come up with more examples on your own.

Which sentence should be deleted?

Ⓐ   2

Ⓑ   3

Ⓒ   4

Ⓓ   5

All of the sentences in this paragraph refer to colors and language except for one. Sentence 4 talks about being sad, which is marginally related to sentence 3, but it does not fit in well with the rest of the paragraph, making it an irrelevant sentence.

EXAMPLE 5

Which of the following sentences should be added to the paragraph?

Ⓐ   In old movies, cowboys in white hats were considered the good guys.

Ⓑ   A whitehead is a type of pimple.

Ⓒ   Adrian White was a brilliant linguist.

Ⓓ   White is a color often associated with absolute terror, as evidenced by phrases such as "white as a ghost."

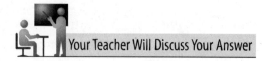 Your Teacher Will Discuss Your Answer

Combining Sentences

Often when you write, you accidentally create sentence fragments, or sentences that do not contain a main clause. Most often, fragments fail to include a subject or verb. When this happens, you need to either add words to make the sentence complete or combine the sentence fragment with another sentence. One common method involves replacing the period in the complete sentence with a comma, adding a joining word such as *and*, *but*, *however*, *including*, or *so*, and then adding the fragment. For example,

Alissa has several hobbies. Karate, skiing, and pottery.

"Karate, skiing, and pottery." is a sentence fragment. To correct it, we combine the full sentence with the fragment.

Alissa has several hobbies, including karate, skiing, and pottery.

sentence – period + comma + joining word + fragment = complete combined sentence

EXAMPLE 6

I like most kinds of cookies. Not chocolate chip, though.

Choose the BEST way to combine this sentence and sentence fragment.

Ⓐ   I like most kinds of cookies not chocolate chip.

Ⓑ   I like most kinds of cookies, not chocolate chip.

Ⓒ   I like most kinds of cookies, and not chocolate chip.

Ⓓ   I like most kinds of cookies, but not chocolate chip.

In choice D the period was replaced with a comma, and the joining word *but* was added. Choice C replaces the period with a comma and adds a joining word, but this sentence does not show the necessary contrast. Choices A and B are simply incorrect.

Another method of combining sentences and sentence fragments involves rephrasing the thought so that the complete sentence and the sentence fragment are combined into one.

Mike's black riding helmet. It was missing last night, but today it is here.

"Mike's black riding helmet." is a sentence fragment. By rephrasing, we can combine the fragment and complete sentence.

Mike's black riding helmet was missing last night, but today it is here.

EXAMPLE 7

Watching cartoons. I was distracted and could not concentrate on my homework.

Choose the BEST way to combine this sentence and sentence fragment, without changing the meaning.

Ⓐ   I watched cartoons until I concentrated on my homework.

Ⓑ   Distracted while watching cartoons, I could not concentrate on my homework.

Ⓒ   I could not concentrate on my homework as I watched cartoons.

Ⓓ   Distracted, I watched cartoons, unable to concentrate on my homework.

Choice B combines the original sentence and fragment without changing the meaning. Choice C fails to state to the reader that the writer is distracted, slightly changing the meaning. Choices A and D each change the meaning of the original sentence and fragment.

Sometimes there are no sentence fragments, but there are several small sentences that read awkwardly. For example:

> *In the summer it is hot. We get sunshine and warm weather. I like to go swimming on hot days.*

These sentences make sense, but they are choppy. To make them read more smoothly, you should combine them, using commas and conjunctions appropriately. For example,

> *I like to go swimming in the summer, when it is hot and we get sunshine and warm weather.*

You may also change, add, and eliminate words when rewriting sentences. Another way of rewriting the three sentences is:

> *During the summer it is hot because of the sunshine, so I get to go swimming.*

Use your best judgment when combining sentences, and be sure that the new sentence has the same essential meaning as the originals.

EXAMPLE 8

Tara is a soccer coach. Her team's name is the Acers. They are the league champions.

Choose the BEST way to combine these sentences.

Ⓐ   Tara is a soccer coach, and her team's name is the Acers, and they are the league champions.

Ⓑ   The Acers is the soccer team that Tara coaches.

Ⓒ   Tara coaches the soccer league champion team, the Acers.

Ⓓ   Tara's team is the Acers, and she is the league champion.

Choice C combines the relevant information from each of the three original sentences and presents it in a cleaner, easier-to-read way. Choice A is incorrect because it reads poorly. Choice B is incorrect because it does not mention that the Acers are the league champions. Choice D is incorrect because it states that Tara, not the team, is the league champion.

Rearranging Words and Sentences

Finally, sometimes the words or sentences you have written are grammatically correct and relevant to what you are saying, but they are not located in the best possible place. For example,

We had fresh salmon for lunch, which we caught in the stream.

In this sentence, there is a misplaced modifier which seems to imply that lunch, rather than the salmon, was caught in a stream. To correct this sentence, you should rearrange the words so that it makes sense.

For lunch, we had fresh salmon, which we caught in the stream.

Now the sentence makes much more sense, and it means what the writer intended it to mean.

EXAMPLE 9

The girl on the desk with colored markers wrote a postcard.

Choose the BEST way to rewrite this sentence.

Ⓐ   The girl wrote a postcard with colored markers on the desk.

Ⓑ   The postcard wrote the girl on the desk with colored markers.

Ⓒ   On the desk, the girl wrote a postcard with colored markers.

Ⓓ   The girl on the desk wrote with colored markers a postcard.

The version of the sentence that makes the most sense indicates that the postcard was written by the girl, that the girl used color markers when writing the postcard, and that it was on the desk when she wrote it. Therefore, choice A works best.

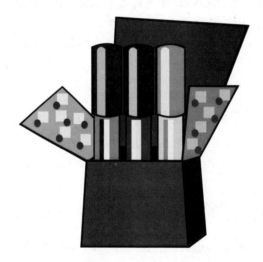

As discussed in chapter 7, sometimes the order of words is appropriate, but the organization of sentences is not. One way to organize sentences is to put them in the order in which events occur. The sentence concerning the first action goes first, the next action appears in the second sentence, and so on.

EXAMPLE 10

(1) Finally, bake them in the oven at 350° for 20 minutes and let them cool. (2) First, gather all the ingredients and grease a pan. (3) It is not difficult to bake chocolate brownies. (4) Next, mix the ingredients together and pour the batter into the pan.

What is the MOST effective order of these sentences?

Ⓐ   1, 2, 3, 4

Ⓑ   4, 3, 2, 1

Ⓒ   1, 3, 2, 4

Ⓓ   3, 2, 4, 1

The correct answer is choice D. The paragraph should read, ·

(3) It is not difficult to bake chocolate brownies. (2) First, gather all the ingredients and grease a pan. (4) Next, mix the ingredients together and pour the batter into the pan. (1) Finally, bake them in the oven at 350° for 20 minutes and let them cool.

Sentence 3 is the topic sentence, which fits best here at the beginning of the paragraph. The order of the next three sentences is 2, 4, 1 because this is the order of the steps to bake brownies. The easiest way to tell which order to put them in is to use the indicating word in each sentence: *first, next,* and *finally.*

Words That Indicate Chronological Order			
first	second	third	fourth
fifth	sixth	seventh	eighth
ninth	tenth	next	then
finally	last	before	after

Not all paragraphs consist of step-by-step instructions, however. In the next example, you need to consider if there is a logical progression of events or thoughts. In other words, ask yourself if the sentences make the most sense in the order in which they are written.

EXAMPLE 11

(1) Despite my self-doubts, I decided to continue. (2) I had done it! (3) With one last shove, I managed to make it to the top. (4) "I'm not going to be able to do it," I thought to myself. (5) "Okay, one … two … THREE!" (6) I had already made a lot of progress, and there wasn't that much farther to go. (7) "What made me think I could carry a sofa upstairs all by myself?"

What is the MOST effective order of these sentences?

Ⓐ   4, 7, 1, 6, 5, 3, 2

Ⓑ   5, 4, 3, 2, 1, 6, 7

Ⓒ   7, 6, 5, 4, 3, 2, 1

Ⓓ   1, 3, 5, 7, 2, 4, 6

The paragraph should read,

"I'm not going to be able to do it," I thought to myself. "What made me think I could carry a sofa upstairs all by myself?" Despite my self-doubts, I decided to continue. I had already made a lot of progress, and there wasn't that much farther to go. "Okay, one … two … THREE!" With one last shove, I managed to make it to the top. I had done it!

Sentence 4 introduces the rest of the paragraph, setting the stage for the events to follow. Sentence 7 follows up on sentence 4 and sets up sentence 1. The rest of the sentences flow logically from one to the next. Sentence 5 flows from 6, and sentences 3 and 2 flow from sentence 5.

Using Correct Vocabulary and a Variety of Words

The word **vocabulary** refers to the kind of words that you use in your writing. When working on your first draft of a paper, you might use very simple words to get an idea across or to help clarify what you want to say. When it is time to revise your paper, though, you want to be sure that you are using appropriate vocabulary for the type of paper you are writing and the audience for whom you are writing. For example, if writing a science paper for a science teacher, be sure to include scientific terms where appropriate. The teacher would be familiar with the terminology, and your use of science terms helps to show that you understand what you are writing about. However, if you were writing for someone that was not familiar with science terms, you would use such terms sparingly, and instead focus on plain-language explanations.

When reviewing your writing, look over your choice of words and think about whether they are appropriate for your paper. You generally want to avoid the use of

- slang
- vulgar or offensive terms
- technical jargon (words that only people in a certain field would understand)
- oversimplified language

EXAMPLE 12

Which of the following sentences do you think would be most appropriate for a general audience?

(A)   Mountain lions, also known as cougars, feed mostly on deer.

(B)   Cougars are hairy, which means they have lots of hair all over their bodies.

(C)   Cougars are mad phat.

(D)   *Felis concolor* is perhaps the most dangerous of the feline genus.

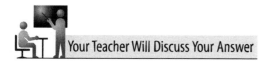 Your Teacher Will Discuss Your Answer

Using a Variety of Words

Using the same words over and over again, or using only very common words, can make your writing seem dull. To make your writing more interesting and inventive, try to use a variety of words when you write.

To help yourself use a greater variety of words, try thinking in more specific terms when writing. Instead of saying that someone sat down, think about how the character would sit. If it is a large, tired old man, for example, perhaps he settled into his chair. A small energetic child might leap into her chair. Someone who is exhausted might collapse onto the sofa. The more specific your thinking, the more precise your word choices will be.

When writing in the first person, consider the voice of the narrator and use words that you think he or she would use. For example, if the narrator was an old southern man talking about a raccoon in his yard, instead of saying "The animal walked out of my yard," he would more likely use words such as "The critter just up and left." A highly sophisticated, wealthy woman talking about her vacation home in Europe would say that she "summered in Paris" rather than that she "took a vacation in France." By thinking about the voice of the narrator (when the narrator is a character in the story), you may find yourself thinking of words that you never would use on your own.

Finally, when you find yourself stuck with a word that you do not want to use, or if you are using the same word over and over again, use a thesaurus to find another word with a similar or more specific meaning. You can also use this resource if you want to come up with a word but can only think of its opposite. In this case, look up the opposite word you are thinking of, and then check to see if there are any antonyms listed. For example, if you are trying to think of a word that means "not dry," look up the word *dry* and check for antonyms. You will likely find words such as *wet, soaked,* and *drenched*.

Regardless of whether you are writing a narrative, a nonfiction report, an article, or any other kind of writing, you should always strive to use a variety of words in your writing. Doing so will make your reading sound more professional, intelligent, and well informed.

EXAMPLE 13

Dave got out of bed and walked into the kitchen to eat. Then Dave walked down the hall, showered, and then Dave got dressed. It was warm out, so Dave walked to work. When Dave got to work, Dave walked to Dave's office and sat in Dave's chair. Dave felt good and Dave knew that Dave was going to have a good day.

Rewrite the passage above, using a greater variety of words to make the passage more interesting. Try to use specific words to make your writing more interesting.

Unit 5   Selections for Practice

Selection 1

This is a student essay on the history of the White House. It contains a number of errors.

The White House

One of the most important and historic addresses in the United States is 1600 Pennsylvania Avenue in Washington, D.C. This is the address of the White House, the official residence and place of business of the president of the United States.

Although George Washington oversaw the construction of the executive residence, it was the country's second president, John Adams, who first lived there. Washington commissioned the design and construction of an illin' new presidential house in 1790, and construction began in 1792. Unfortunately, Washington died in 1799, shortly after leaving office. He died of pneumonia. The building was completed enough to be livable the following year, in 1800.

The building was known as the *President's Palace*, the *President's House*, and the *executive mansion* when it was first built. It did not become known as the White House until nearly twenty years later. During an attack by the British in the War of 1812, the building was set on fire, but it did not burn to the ground. Luckily, a strong rainstorm, which lasted about two hours, was going on when the fire was started. That helped to minimize the damage to the building. When it was repaired, it was covered with a coat of white paynt, at which point it became commonly known as the White House. In 1901, it became formally known by this name. When President Theodore Roosevelt had it engraved on his official stationery.

Go On ➡

There have been many other changes to the structure since it was first built. In 1833, when Andrew Jackson was president, hot water were first piped into the building. Several presidents later, during the tenure of James K. Polk, between 1845-1849, natural gas lines was installed in the White House, allowing the use of gaslights instead of candles for evening illumination. When Indiana native Benjamin Harrison was president (from 1889-1893), electric lights were installed in the executive mansion. Years later, after World War II, President Truman noticed numerous problems with the building and called in professionals to have it inspected. It was determined that there were numerous serious structural defects in the building, and a major overhaul was required. The structural interior was replaced with a steel frame to help shore up the original sandstone walls. During the renovations, Truman and his wife lived across the street in the Blair House.

Today, the White House looks very much the same, on the outside as it did when it was first built. But with each president leaving his own legacy in the building, and regular maintenance and security modifications, the White House is a living, growing, changing building, much like democracy itself.

1a. Which of the following words from this passage is spelled incorrectly?

Ⓐ professionals

Ⓑ paynt

Ⓒ legacy

Ⓓ engraved

1b. Which of the following sentences from this passage is a fragment?

Ⓐ There have been many other changes to the structure since it was first built.

Ⓑ This is the address of the White House, the official residence and place of business of the president of the United States.

Ⓒ It did not become known as the White House until nearly twenty years later.

Ⓓ When President Theodore Roosevelt had it engraved on his official stationery.

Go On

1c. Read this paragraph from the passage.

Although George Washington oversaw the construction of the executive residence, it was the country's second president, John Adams, who first lived there. Washington commissioned the design and construction of an illin' new presidential house in 1790, and construction began in 1792. Unfortunately, Washington died in 1799, shortly after leaving office. He died of pneumonia. The building was completed enough to be livable the following year, in 1800.

Which sentence should be deleted from this paragraph?

Ⓐ   He died of pneumonia.

Ⓑ   Although George Washington oversaw the construction of the executive residence, it was the country's second president, John Adams, who first lived there.

Ⓒ   Washington died in 1799, shortly after leaving office.

Ⓓ   The building was completed enough to be livable the following year, in 1800.

1d. Read this sentence from the passage.

Washington commissioned the design and construction of an illin' new president house in 1790, and construction began in 1792.

Using the Editing Checklist on the following page, rewrite this sentence.

_____

_____

_____

Go On

The Writing Process

> ## *Editing Checklist*
>
> *1* Check your capitalization and punctuation.
>
> *2* Spell all words correctly.
>
> *3* Check for sentence fragments or run-on sentences.
>
> *4* Keep verb tense consistent.
>
> *5* Make sure subject and verb agree.
>
> *6* Use words according to the rules of Standard English.
>
> *7* Remember to paragraph correctly.

1e. Identify TWO note-taking strategies the writer should have used during her research, and explain why she should have done each.

_____

_____

_____

_____

1f. Complete the graphic organizer below, using the information from this passage.

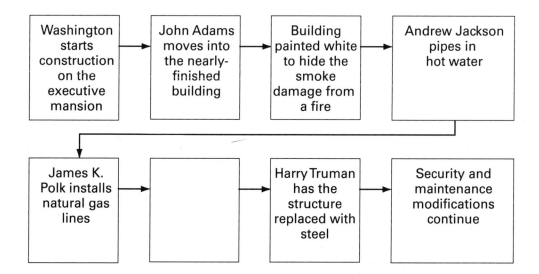

Go On

1g. Create an outline that would be used to prepare for writing this essay.

_____

_____

_____

_____

_____

_____

_____

_____

1h. One of the resources used by the writer was a magazine article titled "The History of the White House" by Joan Adams. It appeared on page 42 of the April 13th issue of *History Magazine,* in 1992. Using this information, prepare a bibliographic citation for this resource.

_____

_____

_____

_____

_____

Go On

Selection 2

Geysers

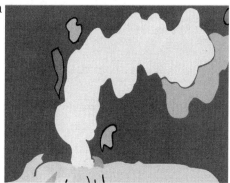

A geyser is a hot spring that shoots water and steam up into the air when the heat from the steam beneath the surface builds up pressure. The firing of the water into the air releases the pressure in a fantastic show of nature. Geysers are extremely rare. They require three components in order to exist: a large supply of water, an intense source of heat (often provided from volcanic activity), and special "plumbing" which allows the heat and water to mix, and which provides an outlet for the explosion of water.

Perhaps the best known geyser in the world can be found in Yellowstone National Park. It is known as Old Faithful because of its dependability. It was given this name in 1870 by the members of a geological expedition who had set up an encampment there. At the time, the geyser seemed to shoot out water for about five minutes every hour. Today, park rangers will tell you that it erupts approximately every 80 minutes. However, it is not as faithful as the name would lead you to believe. In fact, this geyser can erupt anywhere from every 45 minutes to over 100 minutes. The time between eruptions depends on how much water was released in the last spout and how long it lasted.

2a. Which method does the writer use to support his statement that the geyser in Yellowstone National Park is known as Old Faithful because of its dependability?

Ⓐ description of the geyser's location

Ⓑ statistics about the number of times each year the geyser erupts on schedule

Ⓒ anecdote about how it got its name

Ⓓ none of the above

Go On

2b. **What transitional tool is used to link these two paragraphs?**

    Ⓐ   directional transitional words/phrases

    Ⓑ   consequential transitional word/phrases

    Ⓒ   sequential transitional words/phrases

    Ⓓ   details

2c. **Which of the following is the topic sentence of the first paragraph?**

    Ⓐ   A geyser is a hot spring that shoots water and steam up into the air when the heat from the steam beneath the surface builds up pressure.

    Ⓑ   The firing of the water into the air releases the pressure in a fantastic show of nature.

    Ⓒ   Geysers are extremely rare.

    Ⓓ   They require three components in order to exist: a large supply of water, an intense source of heat (often provided from volcanic activity), and special "plumbing" which allows the heat and water to mix, and which provides an outlet for the explosion of water.

2d. **Read these two sentences from the passage.**

Perhaps the best known geyser in the world can be found in Yellowstone National Park. It is known as Old Faithful because of its dependability.

Combine these two sentences into a single sentence without changing their meaning.

_____

_____

_____

_____

_____

Unit 6
Writing Applications

The Indiana Indicators addressed in this unit include:

7.4.2 Students should be able to create an organizational structure that balances all aspects of the composition and uses effective transitions between sentences to unify important ideas.

7.4.3 Students should understand how to support all statements and claims with anecdotes, descriptions, facts and statistics, and specific examples.

7.5.1 Students should be able to write biographical or autobiographical narratives that develop a standard plot line—including a beginning, conflict, rising action, climax, and resolution—and point of view; develop complex characters and a definite setting; and use a range of appropriate strategies, such as dialogue; suspense; and the naming of specific narrative action, including movement, gestures, and expressions.

7.5.2 Students should be able to write responses to literature that develop interpretations that show careful reading, understanding, and insight; organize interpretations around several clear ideas, premises, or images from the literary work; and justify interpretations through sustained use of examples and evidence from the text.

7.5.3 Students should be able to write research reports that pose relevant and focused questions about the topic; communicate clear and accurate perspectives on the subject; include evidence and supporting details compiled through the formal research process, including use of a card catalog, *Reader's Guide to Periodical Literature*, a computer catalog, magazines, newspapers, dictionaries, and other reference books; and document sources with reference notes and a bibliography.

7.5.4 Students should understand how to write persuasive letters or compositions that state a clear position in support of a proposal; describe the points in support of the proposition, employing well-articulated evidence and effective emotional appeals; and anticipate and address reader concerns and counter-arguments.

7.5.5 Students should be able to write summaries of reading materials that include the main ideas and most significant details; use their own words, except for quotations; and reflect underlying meaning, not just superficial details.

7.5.7 Students should be able to write for different purposes and to a specific audience or person, adjusting tone and style as necessary.

GETTING the IDEA

In Unit 6 you will learn how to prepare a narrative, including the basic elements of plot, conflict, rising action, climax, resolution, and setting. You'll learn to reveal your characters through the use of dialogue, movements, gestures, and expressions.

In order to write an effective literary response, you need to understand what you are responding to, develop an argument, and then present it in an effective manner. Unit 6 explains how to interpret what you read, organize your ideas, and use examples and evidence to support your claims.

A research report is an original paper focusing on a specific topic and containing information obtained from several other sources. This unit explains how to use framing questions to establish and develop a topic, use researching strategies to compile your information, and document your sources.

To write an effective persuasive paper, you need to first state your position, then present supporting information. Unit 6 explains these concepts as well as the importance of addressing your reader's concerns and counterarguments.

Finally, Unit 6 discusses writing summaries, including summarizing the main idea of the original work in your own words and including significant details.

Writing Narratives

Plot: Beginning, Conflict, Rising Action, Climax, and Resolution

The plot is the main storyline in a narrative. It is a causal sequence of events, which means that the plot explains why things happen and how each event in the story affects the next event. The majority of the action in the story relates to the plot, and all of the main characters are somehow involved in the plot. The elements of a story's plot are

- beginning
- conflict
- rising action
- climax
- resolution

Beginning

The **beginning** of your plot should act as an introduction, essentially setting up the storyline for the remainder of the story. This part of the story provides exposition, the information that the reader needs to understand the story. It should introduce the main characters, including the protagonist (the main character or "hero" of the story), supporting characters, and the antagonist (the protagonist's opponent, often the "villain" of the story). It should also establish the setting and set the basis for the main conflict, which will be central to the plot.

For example,

> **BEGINNING:** *The story takes place in the recent past, in an average small American town. The main character is Larry Stemple, an average guy working as a clerk in a grocery store. His friends include Tina, another clerk in the store, and Sweeny, an old buddy and regular customer. The antagonist is the store manager, Mr. Berth.*

Conflict

After you establish the beginning of your story and you have introduced the main characters, you should start to establish the main conflict. **Conflict** is the struggle or problem faced by the characters in a story. It may take the form of a single person trying to overcome some problem, two or more people or groups fighting for supremacy, or any other type of struggle. The conflict in a story is often set off by a provoking incident, such as an opportunity being offered, a challenge being laid down, or the introduction of some sort of danger. The conflict will raise certain questions in the reader's mind, such as: *Will this character be successful?* and *What will happen to that character if he/she fails?*

When you determine what the plot of your story will be, you should try to isolate the main conflict that is taking place. This will help you to remain focused on the roles of the characters in your story, and it will help you determine how the narrative begins, develops, and ends. For example,

> **CONFLICT:** *One day while working, Larry sees a notice posted on the office bulletin board. There is another store opening in the town across the river, where Larry actually lives. They are looking for an experienced person to be the manager of the new store. Tina tells him he would be perfect for the job and suggests he ask Mr. Berth for a recommendation. Mr. Berth, however, doesn't particularly like Larry, and he enjoys the power he has over him as his boss. If he recommends him for the job, not only will he not be able to order him around anymore but the two will be considered equals. Worse still, Mr. Berth knows how good a worker Larry is, and how well he would do as a store manager. If Larry gets the job, he could eventually end up as Mr. Berth's boss! He knows he can't simply refuse to submit Larry's name for consideration, so instead he offers him a challenge that Larry could not possibly meet. "Our biggest sales day in history was $10,000, set three years ago on the day before Thanksgiving," he tells Larry. "If you come up with a way to top that sales number in a single day before the end of the month, I'll recommend you for the job."*

Rising Action

The next component of plot is **rising action**. This involves all of the events that lead up to the climax, or final confrontation of the story. When developing the rising action for your story, you illustrate small struggles that lead up to the main struggle or conflict of the story.

The rising action component of the story allows you to flesh out the story and its characters, and it provide clues to the climax and resolution. Two important components of rising action are suspense and foreshadowing.

Suspense involves situations in which there is uncertainty about something. Generally, this means that there is some form of struggle or problem being faced by a character and the reader is unsure of what the outcome will be. The character may face some type of physical danger or be placed into a position where a wrong move could result in his inability to continue on to see the main conflict through to a resolution.

Foreshadowing involves providing clues to how the story will eventually play out. When a writer uses foreshadowing, she gives the reader hints about what will happen later. These clues are often vague, and the reader may not immediately understand them, although when the action plays out, they will be understood. For example, early in a story, one character might tell another that he would do anything for her. Later in the story, when she is in peril, he sacrifices himself to save her. His promise to do anything for her foreshadows his eventual sacrifice for her.

The rising action component generally makes up most of the story, making it the longest single component. Continuing with our story about Larry, here is what a part of the rising action might look like:

RISING ACTION: *Larry and Tina have tried all sorts of ideas to increase business, and sales are up, but nothing close to breaking the one-day sales record. "It's hopeless," Larry tells Tina and Sweeny as the three of them eat breakfast at the local diner. "I'll never make manager."*

"You think you have it bad, kiddo?" asks Sweeny. "Look at this article in the paper. There was a fire at the local food pantry last night. Nobody was hurt, but they lost all of their stock. That food was supposed to feed dozens of people for the rest of the month. They've got problems, buddy. You're not so bad off."

"Yeah, I guess you're right," Larry replied. "At least I still have a job, even if it is working for Mr. Berth ..."

"Larry, that's it!" Tina exclaimed. "The food pantry is empty now, and lots of people know about it because of the news coverage!"

"You're right!" Larry replied. "We can set up some bins in the store for donations, put up some signs, and encourage people to buy and donate!"

"Great idea!" added Sweeny. "I'll call the newspaper and the local radio and television stations. We shouldn't have any problem getting enough people to come in today and buy enough stuff to shatter that sales record!"

Climax

The **climax** of a story is the turning point of the story, often involving the highest dramatic tension. It is in the climax of the story that the main conflict is addressed head-on, and when, generally, one side or the other is victorious. The climax is the part of the story in which the main action takes place, and it is a major turning point for the characters. The climax of Larry's story might look something like this:

CLIMAX: It is the end of the day and the store is almost ready to close. Larry and Tina are adding up the sales receipts for the day. "It's going to be close. We had a lot of business today, but I'm not sure if it was enough," Larry said.

"It just has to be!" Tina exclaimed. "You deserve that job more than anyone else!"

"Oh no!" Larry moaned, moments later. "We're just a few dollars shy of breaking the record, and Mr. Berth is locking the doors now."

The two go downstairs, where Mr. Berth is smiling at them. "Didn't make it, sonny? Aww, that's too bad. I didn't really think you'd pull it off. You never were that smart to begin with, boy. Tell you what, why don't I help you out a bit? I promised the wife I'd bring home some milk for the cats."

"Don't let him get to you, Larry. You did your best. Here, let me ring him out," Tina said. "Oh, Mr. Berth? You know the gallon-sized milk is on sale today. For another dollar you get twice as much as this bottle."

"Oh, you're right, Tina. I'll take that instead," Mr. Berth replied. "Well, sorry, sonny boy, I guess we'll be seeing a lot of each other from now on."

"I don't think so," Larry said. "With that extra dollar, you just pushed our daily sales to $10,000.34. That's a new record, Mr. Berth. I think you owe me a recommendation."

Resolution

The **resolution** of a story is not only how the story ends, but more specifically, how the conflict is resolved and what happens to the characters after the climax. The resolution is designed to answer the question or questions raised by the conflict. In most stories, the conflict is resolved by one character or another being victorious.

One of the most difficult parts of writing a narrative is developing a good ending. Often, writers get so involved in the plot and the development of characters that they forget to work out a good ending. When this happens, a writer can end up creating a weak ending that undermines the rest of the story.

To avoid ending weakly, you should have an idea of how your story will end before you start writing it. You do not have to have all the details necessarily, but you should at least have a plan for ending the story. Take a look at the resolution for Larry's story:

RESOLUTION: *As promised, Mr. Berth recommended Larry for the job, and sure enough, he was hired. Tina came along and became the new store's assistant manager. Larry kept his store so much cleaner and better stocked than Mr. Berth's, and customers enjoyed doing business with him so much that the old store was eventually shut down. Mr. Berth works as a clerk now, in Larry's store, and he certainly regrets being mean to his former employees.*

EXAMPLE 1

Develop a plot for a simple short story, being sure to include the five elements: beginning, conflict, rising action, climax, and resolution.

_____

_____

_____

_____

_____

Setting

Setting is where the story takes place. This is not just the actual geographic location of the story, but is also the time in which it is told, the environment in which it happens, and any other factors (such as "immediately following the funeral of a character's father") that might affect the characters.

As mentioned earlier, setting is part of exposition, which should be identified in the beginning part of the plot. For most stories, the setting will generally be at the beginning, with descriptions of different locations provided as the characters move from place to place throughout the story.

Setting is an important concern for writers because the characters in a story are limited by their environment, the time period in which the story takes place, and so on. The setting for Larry's story might look something like this:

SETTING: *Most of the action in the story takes place in the Nettle Grocery Store, a regional chain food market. The store is a little old and run-down, with slightly dim fluorescent lighting, worn tile floors, and fixtures that are obviously several decades old. The registers are not the modern style with bar code scanners and digital displays, but rather the older, manual style that requires the price of each item to be rung in individually. The office is in a second floor area, just above the registers, overlooking the rest of the store.*

EXAMPLE 2

Determine the setting of your story, based on the plot you developed in the last example. Be sure to include the general time and place in which the story occurs, any specific locations, and the type of environment in which it takes place.

_____

_____

_____

_____

_____

Characterization

Characterization involves the development of characters in a story to help the reader understand who they are, why they behave a certain way, what they believe, and so on. Characterization is an important element that should be used in all forms of writing. The most common tools for characterization are:

- dialogue
- movement, gestures, and expressions

Dialogue

Dialogue consists of conversations between characters or the verbalization of a character's thoughts. When two or more characters are involved in a dialogue, the reader sees how they interact, which helps them to understand the relationship between those characters (whether they genuinely like one another, whether they are enemies, etc.). Character conversations also allow the reader to "hear" what characters are thinking when interacting, and to gain some background about a character (when one character talks about the other's past, for example).

When characters are talking to one another in a narrative, they are also talking to readers, providing information they need to know to further develop their understanding of the characters and their relationship to one another and the plot. Look at some of the dialogue from Larry's story again:

DIALOGUE: *The two go downstairs, where Mr. Berth is smiling at them. "Didn't make it, sonny? Aww, that's too bad. I didn't really think you'd pull it off. You never were that smart to begin with, boy. Tell you what, why don't I help you out a bit? I promised the wife I'd bring home some milk for the cats."*

Mr. Berth's use of terms like *sonny* and *boy* indicate that he is a bit older than Larry and Tina and that he sees himself as being in a position of almost parental authority over the two. His speech indicates a patronizing attitude toward his employees, showing that he considers himself superior to them.

Movement, Gestures, and Expressions

Writers can also reveal character through the physical movements, gestures, and expressions of characters. A character's personality can be reflected in his movements. For example, a very confident and outgoing person would make broad, aggressive movements, whereas a timid character would move slowly and in short steps or keep his head down when meeting people.

Facial expressions are also useful in determining character. A person that is always scowling, for example, is probably unhappy, angry, or resentful. A character that is always smiling is probably generally happy, with a positive outlook on life. A person that is sad will probably look sullen, and a person that is cowardly will probably appear uptight and frightened. Let's see how we could use movement, gestures, and expressions to reveal character in Larry's story:

MOVEMENT, GESTURES, EXPRESSIONS: *As the customers moved through his line, Larry smiled, keying prices into his register as quickly as he could. He stumbled a bit from time to time, and nearly knocked over Mrs. Carter's bag when he swung around to give her her change.*

In this example, Larry's smile shows his optimistic outlook, while his quick actions and clumsiness show that he is a bit nervous.

EXAMPLE 3

Give three examples of characterization for the main character in your story, using dialogue and physical movements or appearances.

_____

_____

_____

_____

_____

_____

_____

Unit 6

Writing Practice

Write a story using the plot you developed in Example 1, the setting you established in Example 2, and the methods of characterization you developed in Example 3.

Be sure to

- include a list showing which point of view, setting, primary conflict, and ending you will use

- show the action rather than merely summarize or explain it

- use a variety of words when telling your story

_____

_____

_____

_____

_____

_____

_____

_____

_____

_____

_____

_____

_____

_____

_____

_____

_____

Writing Applications

Chapter 10 Writing Responses to Literature

Interpreting What You Read

When writing a response to literature, you want your interpretation (your own personal explanation about some aspect of the story) to show that you have carefully read the text you are responding to, that you have understood it, and that you have developed a unique insight into some aspect of it.

The first step is to carefully read the passage or story you are planning to respond to. Read every word and let the information sink in. When you reach the end of a paragraph or a page, take a brief moment to stop and ask yourself if you really paid attention to what you read, and if you understood what was going on. You should be able to identify the characters in the story as well as the primary and secondary plots and subplots. You should also be able to identify the setting, not just where it takes place, but when. If you are unsure, go back to check details.

Another important aspect to reading the text carefully is understanding what you have read—not just the actual events that are happening, but also the motivations of the characters, the potential and actual consequences of events, and so on. Before you prepare a literary response, you should have a thorough knowledge of the story you are responding to, including not only who the characters are and what they did, but why they did what they did and what happened because of it. Failure to understand the story or characters can lead to literary response that is flawed or invalid.

When you respond to literature, you often need to develop interpretations of the actions of characters. While you might think that the actions of characters are self-explanatory, authors often use symbolism, metaphors, and other writing techniques to say something without specifically saying it. There is a message that you should figure out and understand without its being spelled out for you.

When you read, you should pay close attention to the actions of characters, and consider how their actions fit into the rest of the story. Observe what specific characters do, and think about why they are doing what they are doing. Even the simplest actions may be intended to show something more is going on. For example,

Marcus gnawed incessantly on his pencil, turning it a quarter turn each minute to get access to all sides, while Liz twisted and twisted a strand of her hair so many times it stood in a flexed curl on its own when she let go.

What are the characters doing in this sentence? If you only consider the information specifically provided by the narrator, you would say that Marcus chews on a pencil, and Liz twirls her hair with her finger.

As you read this sentence, though, did you get the feeling that more was going on than the narrator was telling you? What do you think is really happening? Why are these characters acting the way that they are?

Now read the rest of the passage.

Then the phone rang. The two stopped and looked at one another for a moment, and then Marcus answered the phone. "Yes?" he said. "Really? That's wonderful! Liz! You have a new grandson!"

As you can see, Marcus and Liz were waiting for a phone call from their son-in-law, telling them that a baby had been born. Marcus and Liz were apparently expecting this call, and were likely nervous. Liz's hair twisting and Marcus's endless pencil-chewing indicate that their actions were not particularly focused, because their minds were elsewhere, thinking about their daughter and the new baby.

The specific actions of the characters were chewing and hair twirling. What was really going on, though, and the true action in this passage, was that the couple was nervously worrying about their daughter and anticipating the phone call. Because the narrator did not tell the reader this, though, you had to interpret it for yourself.

When interpreting a character's actions, think about the character's possible motivations for the actions he or she takes, and then consider which of the possibilities most closely applies to the situation.

EXAMPLE 1

Danny sat silently for a moment, just looking at the two of them. Kathy looked down and away from him. A tear was starting to form in the corner of her eye. Kevin tried looking back at Danny, putting on a strong face, but as soon as their eyes met, he, too, had to turn and look away. "I'm sorry," Kathy said quietly, choking a bit as the tears began to fall.

"So am I," added Kevin, again trying to look at Danny.

"So am I," responded Danny, coldly. With that, he stood up and walked away.

What is MOST LIKELY happening in this passage?

Ⓐ   Danny has just won the lottery.

Ⓑ   Danny has just discovered that his girlfriend is in love with Kevin.

Ⓒ   Kevin and Kathy owe Danny money, but they cannot pay.

Ⓓ   Danny has betrayed Kevin and Kathy.

 Your Teacher Will Discuss Your Answer

Organizing Your Ideas

When you write a response to a story or passage, you express an opinion about some matter related to the narrative, and then develop an explanation that details why you hold your position and provides evidence to support your claims. A literary response should be more than a simple "good" or "bad" statement, but rather a well-organized presentation of your opinions and ideas, containing a thesis statement, supporting paragraphs, and a conclusion.

Thesis Statement

Your thesis is your position on an issue related to a specific work of literature. A **thesis statement**, then, is the sentence or sentences in which you identify the central issue being discussed and present your basic argument. The first part of your thesis statement should briefly state the question or issue you are addressing. For example, let's say you were asked to explain whether or not the two children in the story "Hansel and Gretel" should have entered the house made of candy. Your thesis statement should summarize the issue so that the reader of your essay will know what you are writing about. In the introductory paragraph below, the thesis statement is underlined:

> In the story of Hansel and Gretel, two young children lost in the forest come upon a house made of candy and sweets. They go inside, where they are met by a witch that pretends to be friendly but is actually plotting to kill them. The two manage to escape and kill the witch in the process. Had they not gone inside, they would have remained hungry and could have starved to death. By going inside, though, they were nearly killed and eaten. _I believe it was not wise of the children to enter into an unknown home that was obviously unusual. They should have realized that this was a potentially dangerous situation and gotten out of there._

The first sentences outline the basic storyline of the original narrative so that the reader understands what is being written about. The thesis statement identifies the writer's position on the issue identified in the first part of the paragraph, so now the reader has a strong handle on what the rest of the essay will be about.

Supporting Paragraphs

Supporting paragraphs, which follow the introduction and precede the conclusion, explain your argument in greater detail and provide evidence to support your position. The evidence you include in your supporting paragraphs should contain specific examples from the original text when appropriate and should provide arguments that support your thesis. Also include any relevant information or arguments that are based on prior knowledge when appropriate. Using the Hansel and Gretel example again, a supporting paragraph might look something like this:

These two children had spent their entire lives in or near the forest, and in all that time, they had never come across a house made of sweets. In fact, it is quite likely that they had never even heard of such a thing existing. Therefore, when they came upon it, they should have been suspicious of what they were seeing. While I would not expect them to ignore it completely, they should have known enough not to eat parts of the structure, and they certainly should have been alarmed enough to know that going inside would be a bad idea. When a hunter wants to trap a bear, he sets a trap and puts bait into it. The bear does not know enough to realize that the steel jaws of a trap are not normally found in its habitat, so it is easily trapped. Humans, even children, are smarter than bears and should know enough to be able to recognize when something seems too good to be true.

As you can see, this paragraph makes references to events and situations in the story and also draws on outside knowledge to make an appropriate comparison. Additional supporting paragraphs would present similar arguments in similar ways.

Conclusion

The **conclusion** of a literary response, like conclusions to other types of writing, is meant to bring the essay to a close. When preparing your conclusion, you should be sure to briefly restate your argument and basic points. Try not to make your conclusion too long or too similar to your introduction. Remember, by the time you get to the conclusion, the reader is aware of what you have to say. Do not include new information in the conclusion; just summarize your argument and basic points, and end.

The conclusion to the Hansel and Gretel example would look something like this:

> *While it is understandable that Hansel and Gretel would be interested in a house made of candy, they should have been suspicious of such an unusual structure in a relatively familiar environment, and they should have been smart enough not to willingly go into a stranger's home. Instead, they should have chosen a path and continued moving forward, which would have likely brought them to some form of civilization sooner or later. The lesson here is, don't go into strange houses—you might not come back out!*

EXAMPLE 2

Write a thesis statement in response to a story you have read, then describe TWO types of evidence you could give to support your claim. Then write a conclusion.

_____

_____

_____

_____

_____

_____

_____

_____

_____

_____

_____

_____

Using Examples and Evidence

When responding to literature, you make some type of claim or present some form of argument or opinion. In order for the reader to take you seriously, though, you need to provide some examples and/or evidence from the story to back up your claim.

Using the Hansel and Gretel example again, you would want to include examples of information from the story that indicated why going inside was a bad idea. This might include the description of the setting in which the children's home was located and any descriptions of their previous trips into the forest. This could be used to contrast with the descriptions of the candy house, to show how out-of-place this structure was in the forest.

Early in the story, the mother talks to the father about leaving the children in the forest, saying, "We will take the children out into the forest to where it is the thickest; there we will light a fire for them, and give each of them one more piece of bread, and then we will go to our work and leave them alone." This statement implies that it was not unusual for the family to go out into the woods together and for the children to be left alone. If this is true, then the children should be familiar with the normal features of the woods. When they reached the witch's house, though, they found "it was built of bread and covered with cakes, but that the windows were of clear sugar." They should have realized that such a structure was not normally found in the forest.

Including these specific descriptions in the passage makes the point that the children should have been familiar with the forest and realized that the house was suspicious, but did not, indicating poor judgment.

EXAMPLE 3

Provide a specific example of supporting evidence based on your response to Example 2, and write a paragraph that supports your thesis statement.

_____

_____

_____

_____

_____

_____

_____

_____

_____

_____

_____

_____

_____

_____

_____

_____

_____

_____

Unit 6

Writing Practice

Read the writing prompt below, and complete the writing activity.

The Gold Nugget
a traditional tale of Syria

Long ago, there lived a small family consisting of a father, a mother, and a young son. For many years, the father worked on their small farm, making just enough of a living so that the family could get by. As his son grew up, the aging man told him that one day he would have to go out into the world and make his own way. He also told him that he would need to support his parents, who would be too old to take care of themselves.

Finally, that day came. The old man called his grown son into the room, telling him, "You have become a young man and now you must go out and get work and support your mother and me. Leave our house today, and do not return until you have earned a gold nugget!"

The old man's wife overheard their conversation and was saddened. She did not want her son to leave them, so when he came out of the room, she gave him one of her only two gold nuggets. "Present this to your father, and perhaps he will let you stay."

The son brought the nugget to his father, who examined it and then threw it out the window, telling him, "This nugget is too small. Go away and do not come back until you have a larger nugget."

The mother heard what happened, and then gave the boy the other nugget, which was a little bigger. Unfortunately, it was not big enough to please the old man, who threw it out the window.

Crushed, the son finally decided to go into town and to work to earn his own gold nugget. He worked very hard for quite awhile, until he was finally able to afford to buy his own gold nugget, which was actually much smaller than the nuggets he had earlier shown his father.

When the father saw the nugget, he said, "Too small," and headed toward the window to throw it out. Realizing what was about to happen, the son leapt up and snatched the nugget from the old man's hand before he could throw it away. Smiling, the old man looked at his son and said, "Congratulations, today you are a real man! Keep your gold nugget, for it is really yours."

Go On

Why do you think the old man called his son a real man at the end of this story? Write an essay in which you explain why the old man did what he did, and why you believe the son became a man that day.

Be sure to

- clearly state your position
- provide evidence to support your position
- include at least two supporting paragraphs
- include a beginning, middle, and ending to your essay
- review your writing for correct paragraphing, grammar, spelling, punctuation, and use of Standard English

_____

_____

_____

_____

_____

_____

_____

_____

_____

_____

_____

_____

_____

_____

_____

STOP

Writing Research Reports

Framing Questions

Framing questions are questions you ask yourself in order to direct your investigation when writing a research report. The answers to your framing questions will help you establish the parameters (boundaries) for your research, identifying the specific information you should look for and write about.

Every time you ask a framing question, you can ask another framing question based on the answer. For example, let's say that you need to write a research paper about an important historical figure. Examples of framing questions and answers might be these:

Question: *Which historical figures do I know about?*

Answer: *I am familiar with George Washington, Christopher Columbus, Leonardo da Vinci, Abraham Lincoln, Benjamin Franklin, Queen Victoria, Socrates, and Thomas Edison.*

Question: *Which of these people do I know the most about?*

Answer: *I am most familiar with Thomas Edison.*

Question: *Should I write a complete biography or focus on one part of his life?*

Answer: *I am supposed to write a five-page paper, so I would not have enough space to write a complete biography. I should focus on just one part of his life.*

Question: *Which part of his life will I focus on?*

Answer: *He is most well known for his inventions, so I will focus on his career as an inventor.*

Question:	*Which inventions in particular do I want to include in my paper?*
Answer:	*I will write about his work with the light bulb, the phonograph, and the motion-picture camera.*

As you can see, these five questions quickly brought the research topic into focus, from a very general topic to a relatively specific topic. It would also be possible to continue on from this point, asking more framing questions to bring the topic into even greater focus. You should continue your framing questions until you have reached an appropriate place from which to begin your research. Do not stop too early, or you will end up researching too broad a topic. However, you should also avoid asking too many questions, as your research might be more focused than desired. For example, if you continued to ask questions about this topic, you might eventually end up writing a paper focused entirely on a single decision Edison made!

EXAMPLE 1

Your assignment is to write a three-page paper about a national monument. What should your first framing question be?

Ⓐ   Where did the Statue of Liberty come from?

Ⓑ   Which Roosevelt is on Mount Rushmore?

Ⓒ   Which national monument do I know the most about?

Ⓓ   Who designed the Washington Monument?

This question in choice C involves asking yourself which national monument you are most familiar with. You want to write a paper about something you already know something about, because you won't have to spend as much time doing research. The other three choices are incorrect because they are too specific to act as a starting point.

EXAMPLE 2

Suppose that you've decided to write about the Statue of Liberty. What would your next framing question be?

Ⓐ   What is the significance of the Statue of Liberty?

Ⓑ   What does the inscription at its base say?

Ⓒ   When was the Statue of Liberty last renovated?

Ⓓ   Where can I buy a miniature replica of the Statue of Liberty?

The purpose of framing questions is to bring your research into focus. Determining the significance of the Statue of Liberty will help you hone in on the exact topic you will write your paper on.

EXAMPLE 3

You have decided that you are going to focus your paper on the fact that the Statue of Liberty was a gift to the United States from the nation of France. What would be your next framing question?

Ⓐ   How long did it take for the Statue to make the journey across the ocean?

Ⓑ   Are the French still happy that they gave us the Statue?

Ⓒ   In which part of France was the Statue made?

Ⓓ   Why did France give us the Statue?

Again, you want to increasingly focus your research based on your previous answer to a framing question. The answer to the question "Why did France give us the Statue?" would identify the specific reasons we were given the gift, which is where you want to focus your research.

Establishing and Developing a Topic

When you first decide on a general topic to write about, or when you are first given a general writing assignment, you must determine exactly what you will write about. Using framing questions will help you refine your topic and direct your research. After you have asked your framing questions and have decided what to write about, you will need to develop your topic with simple facts, details, examples, and explanations.

Facts

Facts are bits of information that are generally accepted as true. Examples of facts include: "The sky is blue"; "Abraham Lincoln was a U.S. president"; and "Water is made up of hydrogen and oxygen." They differ from opinions, which vary from person to person. Examples of opinions include: "Joey is the best basketball player ever"; "Cindy is nicer than Melanie"; and "That is not funny."

When developing your topic, you should focus on looking for and presenting facts. While your paper may include your own opinions, they should be backed up with facts, not the opinions of others. For example, if in your paper you were arguing that Benedict Arnold should not have been branded a traitor during the Revolutionary War, you would want to support your position with facts about Arnold and the situation he was in. You would not want to say that Arnold should not have been branded a traitor because a particular historian said so.

Details

Details take a general idea or statement and make it more specific. When developing your topic, you should include as many details as appropriate. Avoid having too general a topic, which would make it difficult to cover every aspect successfully. You also need to be careful not to have too specific a topic, which can limit your scope too much. Your topic should be detailed enough that it allows you to focus your research and writing into an appropriate number of pages, but not so detailed that your focus goes far beyond what was originally intended.

Examples

When researching and preparing to write about your topic, you should look for **examples** related to the points you are making. For example, the statement "Porcupines can be dangerous" is broad, and it leaves it up to the reader to determine how dangerous porcpines can be. However, if you add examples, you can clarify your meaning.

> *Porcupines can be dangerous creatures. For example, the thousands of barbed quills of the North American porcupine detach easily and can cause severe pain when lodged in an attacker's skin. They can sometimes even cause death if they puncture a vital organ or if the incision they cause becomes infected.*

Specific examples make it easier for the reader to understand the point you are trying to make.

Explanations

Anytime you make a point, you should include an **explanation**, even if it is only a simple one. You should not assume that the reader will always understand what you are talking about. When you write a paper, you are explaining a topic to the reader, so it is your responsibility to provide an adequate explanation. For example, if you are writing a paper that you were going to read to your class, instead of saying

> *Canines are considered the most domesticated animal, next to felines.*

you would want to say something along the lines of

> *Of all animals with the exception of felines (cats), canines (dogs), are considered to be the most domesticated.*

190

EXAMPLE 4

You are writing a report on soccer. Which of the following is a FACT that you might use in your paper?

Ⓐ   Metal cleats are the best shoes to wear when playing soccer.

Ⓑ   Soccer is the number one spectator sport in many countries.

Ⓒ   Soccer should be played only by adults because it is a dangerous sport.

Ⓓ   There are no referees in the game of soccer.

Choice B is a known fact that could be proven. Choices A and C are incorrect because they are opinions.
Choice D is incorrect because it is a false statement, which is neither a fact nor an opinion.

EXAMPLE 5

Which of the following statements is the MOST detailed?

Ⓐ   There are lots of animals in the world.

Ⓑ   Cats are a type of animal.

Ⓒ   There are many types of cats, such as tabbies.

Ⓓ   The American Wirehair is an unusual breed of cat that is believed to have mutated spontaneously and exists, only in the United States.

 Your Teacher Will Discuss Your Answer

EXAMPLE 6

Which statement is MOST LIKELY to require an additional example and/or explanation when included in a report?

Ⓐ   The U.S. Space Agency is studying how to recycle water in space.

Ⓑ   Water freezes when it gets too cold.

Ⓒ   Fish live underwater.

Ⓓ   People need to drink water to survive.

Not everyone knows what goes into recycling water, and this statement seems to imply that the writer will continue on, explaining how water will be recycled in space, and why such a process is necessary. Choices B, C, and D are all general statements that most people would be able to understand, so no further examples or explanations would normally be necessary.

Researching

When you are researching your topic, you should never rely on one single source for all of your information because that source may not have the most current information, may be unreliable, or may not adequately provide the information you are looking for. It is usually best to use several reference sources, such as:

- books—Textbooks and other works of nonfiction written by experts in a particular field of study

- encyclopedias—These multi-volume reference sets are often the most thorough resource for topics you might be researching.

- articles from reputable publications—Before using an article as a reference, be sure that it was published by an organization that is considered reliable. For example, the *New York Times* newspaper and *Time* magazine would be considered reputable sources, whereas tabloid newspapers, which sometimes publish stories about aliens and supernatural events, would not.

Each of these three types of resources can be found at your local or school library. The easiest and most common way to find the information you are looking for is to search by topic. This means you should look up terms related to the topic you are writing about. If you were writing about dogs, for example, you might look up terms such as *dog, canine, mammal,* or *beagle.*

You can search for books related to your topic by using the card catalog or, if they have one, the library's computerized search program. If you look up terms related to your topic, either of these tools will provide you with a list of books and the codes indicating where they can be found on the shelf.

If you want to search for articles related to your topic, your library probably has a reference book called the *Reader's Guide to Periodical Literature.* This is a publication which lists articles written about specific topics within a certain period of time, and it provides information about where and when they were published. To use the *Reader's Guide,* look up the topic in the main directory, and then go through the list of related articles. Then, using the information you found, go through the library's collection of periodicals (magazines and journals) to locate the issue you are looking for. Ask your librarian to help if you are having trouble.

Encyclopedias are easy to use and are organized into alphabetized volumes. To find information in an encyclopedia, go to the volume containing your search term or topic, and then find the related entry.

In addition to these traditional reference sources, there are a number of electronic resources that are also available today, including:

- search engines
- online directories
- web sites
- reference books on CD-ROM

If you have ever used the Internet, you have probably used a **search engine**, a special type of Web site that searches other Web sites to locate information related to a topic. To use a search engine, you merely type in your search term, and then review the results and click on the links that seem most relevant to what you are looking for.

Online directories are very much like search engines, but rather than give you a list of all Web sites containing information related to your topic, they provide you with a list of sub-topics and directories of sites that might be related to your topic. This allows you to locate more specific information about part of your topic more easily and faster.

Search engines and online directories both point you to Web sites which contain information related to your search terms. You must always be very careful when using Web sites for research. Just as with articles, you need to consider the source of your information before relying on it as fact. Sites that generally contain reliable information include:

- government Web sites (any Web address ending with *.gov*)
- college and university Web sites (any Web address ending with *.edu*)
- official Web sites of reputable news organizations
- official Web sites of reputable professional organizations and not-for-profits (sometimes ending with *.org*)

Many traditional reference books, such as encyclopedias and dictionaries, are also available as CD-ROMs. These work very much like search engines in that after you have put the disc in your computer and installed the program, you merely need to type in your search terms and then click on the related entries.

EXAMPLE 7

Which resource should you use to find an article published in the August 13 issue of *Newstime* magazine in 1974?

(A) standard print edition of *Encyclopedia Britannica*

(B) *Reader's Guide to Periodical Literature*

(C) CD-ROM version of *Encyclopaedia Britannica*

(D) Princeton University Web site

The *Reader's Guide* is a tool which you can use to locate articles printed in periodicals such as magazines and trade journals.

EXAMPLE 8

You are trying to find information about cacti, but your searches have not turned up many results. Which term should you try instead of "cacti"?

(A) desert plants

(B) Banel Cactus

(C) pines

(D) plants

If you are not finding enough information using a specific search term, you should try a slightly more general term. In this case, the more general term is "desert plants." This search would probably lead you to resources that contain information about all types of desert plants, including cacti. Choice B is incorrect because Banel Cactus is a specific type of cactus, meaning that using this term would be a more refined search rather than a more general search. Choice C is incorrect because pines are a different type of plant altogether, and choice D is incorrect because it is too general a term and would likely result in resources about not only cacti, but all types of plants from various climates.

EXAMPLE 9

Which of the following would be the MOST reliable source of information about the stock market?

Ⓐ   *America First!*—www.americafirst.org

Ⓑ   FBI Web site—www.fbi.gov

Ⓒ   *Quick-E-Traderz* cheap and easy stock trades—www.quicknet.com

Ⓓ   The *Wall Street Journal* Web site—www.wsj.com

The Wall Street Journal is recognized as the industry leader for financial news, and it has a long history of providing solid, factual information. Choice A is incorrect because it is an organization Web site, most likely devoted to American firms, meaning it may be biased in its presentation of news. Choice B is incorrect because the FBI is a law enforcement agency, not a financial institution. Choice C is incorrect because it is a business that is likely not reputable, meaning they might be willing to tell you anything in order to make a quick sale.

Documenting Sources

Researching is a vital component of preparing any research paper. When you research, you take information obtained from other sources and include it in your own work. Because you are not the original author or researcher who discovered or verified the information you are including, you must be sure to make a notation indicating where the information came from. This is done not only so that the person reading your paper can verify your claims, but also so that the person or people who prepared the publications you used as references receive due credit.

As you learned in Chapter 7, the two most common tools for making such notations are endnotes and bibliographic references. Endnotes are used to reference individual claims, facts, and statistics, and a bibliography provides a complete list of all references used when researching your paper.

To review:

Endnotes are a list of sources used in researching a paper, found toward the end of the report. Each reference to an outside source made in the body of the paper must be reflected in an endnote.

When making a reference to a source in the body of the paper, you should provide a number which corresponds with the numbered endnote. The number should be slightly raised in comparison to the other text, so that the reader knows that it is intended as a citation. For example,

During the Civil War, 5,867,000 Americans lost their lives.[5]

This notation indicates that the source of this information can be found in endnote number 5.

A bibliography is the list of resources used in researching a paper. Unlike endnotes, which cite specific pages where specific tidbits of information were found, the bibliography lists all of the books, magazines, etc., the author used.

Like endnotes, a bibliography uses a standardized format that must always be followed. The bibliographic references are not numbered to coincide with citations within the body of the work. Instead, they are organized alphabetically, by the first letter in the first major word in each citation. Review Chapter 7 for formatting procedures for endnotes and bibliographic entries.

It is vitally important to always include endnotes and a bibliography in all research papers that you prepare. Failure to reference resources used when researching your paper may be considered a copyright violation.

EXAMPLE 10

You should include endnotes when writing

Ⓐ   a literary research paper

Ⓑ   a scientific research paper

Ⓒ   a mathematics research paper

Ⓓ   any type of research paper

Regardless of the topic of your paper or the subject for which it is written, all research papers should reference resources.

EXAMPLE 11

The citations in your bibliography should be arranged

Ⓐ   from most recent to oldest

Ⓑ   from oldest to most recent

Ⓒ   alphabetically

Ⓓ   by resource type

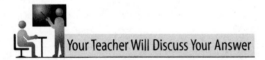
Your Teacher Will Discuss Your Answer

Writing Practice

This exercise will test your ability to perform the processes described in this chapter.

Part I

Choose one of the following four topics

- Animals
- Weather
- History
- Medicine

Part II

For the topic you chose, write and answer FOUR framing questions to focus your research.

_____

_____

_____

_____

_____

_____

_____

_____

_____

_____

Go On

Part III

Identify your specific topic.

_____

_____

_____

_____

_____

Part IV

Identify FOUR resources you could use to research your topic, and for each, explain how you would go about finding the resource.

_____

_____

_____

_____

_____

When answering, be sure to

- answer each of the four parts
- specify the general topic you chose
- give an answer for each of your framing questions
- use the answer from your previous framing question to ask your next framing question
- specify the specific topic you would write about

STOP

Writing Persuasive Letters or Compositions

Stating Your Position

The purpose of writing a persuasive letter or composition is to convince the reader to agree with your opinion on an issue. The first step in developing a persuasive paper, then, is to identify the question or issue that you are discussing, and then you should state your position. For example, if you were writing about an upcoming ballot initiative which asked the voters to decide whether to allow casino gambling in the state, your opening paragraph might look something like this:

> *In a few weeks, the voters of this state will go to the polls to answer the question of whether or not casino gambling parlors should be opened in this state. It is my firm belief that this measure should be voted down, and that this state should be kept casino-free. A state free of gambling is a state with greater freedom.*

You should always start off a persuasive letter or essay by stating your position in order to help the reader to understand what you are writing about. You want the reader to know what point you are trying to make, so you should be sure that you state your position clearly. Also be sure to review your opening statement after you have written it, to be sure that your reader will not be confused about your stance on the issue.

It is also important to remember to structure your argument in positive terms. This means you should always present your argument as being in favor of something, rather than against something. For example, in the example above, instead of arguing against allowing casinos, the writer is arguing to keep the state casino-free. In this sense, the author is arguing for something rather than against something. It is easier to convince a person to do something than not to do something. To illustrate this point, read this version of the previous example, re-written in negative terms rather than positive.

> *In a few weeks, the voters of this state will go to the polls to answer the question of whether we should allow casino gambling in this state. I feel that we should not allow casinos to open in this state. A state that allows gambling is a state that allows its citizens to be robbed.*

Think about how you felt after reading each version of this opening statement. Did you feel better after reading the first example or the second? Chances are that the second one jumped out at you a bit more, but the first one probably left you feeling more secure about the writer and his or her argument. The second one more likely made you feel almost as if you were being attacked, and likely left you wondering about the writer's motives.

Positive, supportive language is more likely to encourage the reader to come away from your writing with a positive image of what you had to say. Negative language, though, leaves the reader feeling negatively. Also, when you write in a negative manner, you are constantly addressing the thing you are against. This means that readers go away from your passage thinking less about what you want them to do, and more about what you do not want them to do. Your goal in persuasive writing is to get the reader thinking about what you are arguing for, not what you are arguing against.

EXAMPLE 1

Choose the BEST statement to include in a persuasive letter being sent to members of a group who are trying to decide where to build their new headquarters.

Ⓐ   Miami has too much crime, so we shouldn't build there.

Ⓑ   This organization doesn't do anything of any great importance.

Ⓒ   Philadelphia would be a good location because of the city's cultural diversity and historical significance.

Ⓓ   If you are intelligent like me, then you know where you should stand on this issue.

The statement in choice C clearly identifies the writer's position, and it uses positive language. Choice A is incorrect because it uses negative language, although it does clearly identify the writer's opinion. Choice B is incorrect because it uses negative language and it does not clearly state a position about the question at hand. Choice D is incorrect because the reader is left feeling uncertain about what the writer's opinion is.

Supporting Your Position

After you have stated your position, you need to support it in order to try to persuade others to feel the same way. The two most effective tools for doing this are:

- relevant evidence
- effective emotional appeals

Relevant evidence includes any information that is related to the issue and that supports the position you are taking. For example, if you were arguing in favor of recycling in your community, relevant evidence would include information about how much money other cities and towns have saved over time by instituting a recycling program, how a great number of the people in your community support a recycling program, and how much cleaner the community would be if people recycled.

If the evidence is not relevant, even though it might be compelling, it will not significantly help your case. In fact, introducing evidence that is irrelevant could serve to backfire if the reader interprets its inclusion as a sign of the writer's lack of knowledge and understanding about the issue. For example, if, when making your argument in favor of recycling, you wrote about the need for manufacturers to make more products out of recycled materials, readers could be confused, or worse, they might assume that you are an environmental extremist who is more concerned about your own agenda than about the community. When providing evidence to support your position, stay focused on the purpose of your composition.

People do not make decisions based entirely on what they think. They often decide to do or not to do something based, at least in part, on the way they feel. For this reason, you should also include effective emotional appeals when appropriate. Using the recycling example again, you might include an emotional appeal which seeks a return to a simpler time when people cared about their community and worked hard to keep it clean, or an appeal to live up to their parents' and grandparents' values and hopes and dreams for the community. You could also express it as a wish for the future in which your children will have a cleaner, safer place to live, where they have grown up with strong convictions and a work ethic that does not allow the wasting of resources that can be reused.

When you make an emotional appeal, you address the reader's heart, not just his or her mind. When trying to convince someone to agree with your position, you can succeed with the right emotional appeal.

EXAMPLE 2

You are writing a composition in which you state you are in favor of increasing financial aid to schools in low-income areas. Which of the following would NOT be considered relevant evidence?

Ⓐ   Low-income communities have lower property values, so those school districts do not get as much money from property taxes.

Ⓑ   Students are often disinterested in the source of financing for their school.

Ⓒ   Schools in low-income areas have less money to spend on vital materials, such as books and computers.

Ⓓ   Tax increases will not solve the problem because most people in low-income areas do not have the money to pay higher taxes.

While it may be true that students do not think about where the money to fund their school comes from, it does not directly apply to the issue being discussed. Choices A, C, and D all relate specifically to the issue at hand and support the writer's position.

EXAMPLE 3

In the same composition, which of the following would be an effective emotional appeal to persuade people to support an increase in financial aid to schools in low-income areas?

Ⓐ   Using money more effectively could reduce the amount of additional funds needed in these schools.

Ⓑ   A tax increase in a low-income community might result in fewer people paying their taxes.

Ⓒ   Children cannot control the circumstances in which they must live, but together, we can help give them the opportunities they need to succeed and to make something of their lives.

Ⓓ   Increased aid to these schools would require increased taxes for everyone else in the state.

The statement in choice C appeals to the reader's emotions about innocent children that have to make do with less. It speaks to the reader's heart more so than to his or her mind. Choices A and B provide relevant evidence to support the argument, but they are not focused on appealing to the reader's heart. Choice D is incorrect because it argues against increased financial aid, rather than for it.

Addressing Your Reader's Concerns and Counterarguments

One of the most important things to remember when writing a persuasive letter or composition is that your argument has to address your reader's concerns. If the issue you are addressing is not relevant to the reader, he or she will not care what you have to say. For example, if you were writing a letter that was going to be read to a group of preschoolers, you would not want to write about financing a mortgage. The issue you speak about, and the position you take, should be relevant to the reader's interests.

Even if the issue you are addressing is relevant to your reader, you must remember to address his or her concerns regarding the issue. To do this, first consider the supporting evidence and emotional appeals you can make to support your position, and then identify which of your points the reader is most likely to be interested in. Generally speaking, people are most interested in things that concern them in some way. When you can align what you want to say with the interests of your reader, you are most likely to be successful in the argument you are trying to make.

Another way to approach the problem of trying to address your reader's concerns is to think about the issue you will be writing about, and then identify how that issue will most likely affect your readers. For example, let's say that you are preparing a paper to be read to a community group. In your composition, you are going to speak out against building a strip mall in a location where there is currently a park. What do you think your audience will be most concerned about?

In this case, the readers are most likely to be interested in how building a strip mall would affect them. If you are taking a position against building the mall, you should think about the negative effects that would be experienced by the community. For example, building the mall will mean losing the park. You could argue that the community has too few natural spaces as it is, or that losing the park will deprive children of a safe place to play. Also, where there are stores, there are customers. This means that there will be more traffic in the area where the mall will be built, which will mean more noise, more pollution, and a greater danger of automobile accidents.

You also have to consider the positive benefits of the issue you are discussing, and try to find ways to argue against them. Keep in mind that your reader may be in favor of what you are against. This means that you will have to find a way to change his or her mind. For example, building a strip mall will mean new businesses moving into the area. This means that there will be more tax money for the community to spend, and the new stores will be convenient for residents. So what can you do to speak out against these benefits?

In regard to the increased taxes, while this means that more money will be made available to the community, the new strip mall will also mean more expenses. The community will need to pay for additional lighting in the area, extra security, and road maintenance. The mall will also drain resources, such as the local water and energy supply. You could argue that the amount of money brought in to the community by building the mall would not be as great as the cost to the community of having the mall.

As for convenience, the stores moving into the mall might be national chain stores. You could make an emotional appeal to readers, arguing that shopping at these stores would put local small storeowners out of business, destroying the heart of the community and ruining its small-town image.

EXAMPLE 4

You are writing an essay in which you want to persuade a plumbers' union to support a proposed state law that would require stricter code enforcement for new structures. Which of the following would be of the GREATEST concern to plumbers in this regard?

Ⓐ   New plastic pipes are often used instead of traditional metal pipes when making repairs.

Ⓑ   Lawmakers vote on a variety of state laws throughout the legislative session.

Ⓒ   Gravity causes water to naturally flow down toward the ground.

Ⓓ   Passage of the law would mean that more reliable pipes and connectors would have to be installed in new buildings.

If you are writing to persuade the plumbers to support the law, then you must address how the law will affect them. By telling them that passage of the law would mean that more reliable pipes and connectors would have to be installed in new buildings, they will clearly understand what the law would mean to them, helping them to come to a decision. While the other choices are marginally related to the issue, they do not provide any new or relevant information to the intended audience.

Addressing Counterarguments

One of the most effective methods of persuading readers is to anticipate their counter-arguments and address them accordingly. A counterargument is an argument a person who opposes your position would make in response to your argument. For example, let's say that you are writing a letter to persuade the city government to use a tax surplus to improve the city's infrastructure rather than to reduce taxes. Your main point would be that the money could be used to provide new, up-to-date equipment for city departments and to replace aging water lines.

What you would need to do at this point would be to consider the viewpoint of your opposition, and think about how they would react to your argument. What would they say?

The most likely counterargument would be that the budget surplus came from people being taxed too much, and that the money rightfully belongs to the taxpayers. To make your argument stronger, you should address this counterargument in your presentation. For example,

To those who would argue that the surplus should be restored to the taxpayers, I would respond that investing in the city's infrastructure will save the taxpayers far more in the long run than a small, temporary tax reduction would save them now. By replacing the city's aging main water line, we will mostly eliminate the need for regular repairs, which currently cost the city tens of thousands of dollars each year in materials and overtime. It will also provide us with more time and flexibility in replacing the line than it would if we waited until it completely burst, at which point all water would have to be shut off, and the roads would need to be torn up to get to the line. By acting proactively, we can work in stages, saving both time and money, and providing a greater benefit to the residents of this city than any tax cut could ever hope to give.

By anticipating your opponent's counterarguments, you can address their concerns and develop a much stronger persuasive paper.

Read the writing prompt below and complete the writing activity.

Your town has experienced a major population growth over the last ten years. Along with the growth in the number of residents has come a sizeable increase in the amount of garbage filling up the landfill. In response to the problem, some residents have suggested using a one-time government grant to purchase an incinerator that would reduce the large piles of trash to small piles of ash. Others want to use the money to establish a recycling program.

Write a persuasive essay in which you argue for either purchasing an incinerator or establishing a recycling program.

Be sure to

- identify why you are writing the essay and the position you are taking
- provide relevant evidence and/or emotional appeals to support your position
- organize your argument, making your strongest points first
- address the concerns of your audience

_____

_____

_____

_____

_____

_____

_____

_____

_____

_____

Go On

_____

_____

_____

_____

_____

_____

_____

_____

_____

_____

_____

_____

_____

_____

_____

_____

_____

_____

_____

_____

_____

_____

Writing Applications

Chapter 13

Writing Summaries

Summarizing Main Idea and Significant Details

When writing, you will often need to refer to other written materials. In doing so, it would not be practical to rewrite the text you are referring to, and in many cases, doing so would constitute a copyright violation. When referring to, or responding to, another written piece, it is best to summarize.

A **summary** is a short piece, ranging from a sentence to several paragraphs, in which you recall the main points of another piece of writing using your own words rather than copying the original text word for word. It is designed to help your reader quickly grasp the original passage that you are referring to without having to read it or otherwise be familiar with it.

When summarizing reading materials, you should only include the main idea and the most significant details. Simply focus on what the story or article is about, and include only those details which are of significance. For example, let's say that you needed to provide a summary of the story "Snow White", from *Grimm's Fairy Tales*. Rather than explain the full story and all of its components, you would want to focus on the main plot and important details. A summary would look something like this:

> *"Snow White" is the story of a young girl who is driven from her home by her evil stepmother, who attempts to have her killed. Fleeing to the forest, the young girl comes upon the home of seven dwarves, whom she befriends. When her stepmother gets word that the girl still lives, she seeks her out and tricks her into biting a poisoned apple, which causes her to fall into a deep, mystical sleep. Finding her and thinking her dead, the dwarves place her into a glass coffin, believing her too beautiful to place into the ground. Soon after, a prince comes upon the coffin, opens it, and kisses the girl, breaking the spell and awakening her. The two marry and live happily ever after.*

As you can see, the story that would have filled many pages in its full form has been broken down here into its primary elements, taking up only a paragraph. The way in which you summarize reading material will vary a bit, depending on your purpose. If you were writing a paper about trespassing in fairy tales, for example, you would focus more on Snow White's entry into the dwarves' home. The main thing to remember is that you should focus on the main idea of the written piece you are referring to and the details that are either significant to the story or significant to your own topic.

EXAMPLE 1

Read the following passage, and then answer the questions that follow.

Glaciology is the study of glaciers, giant slow-moving masses of ice that are formed on land. This science also covers the general study of ice and natural phenomena that involve ice. For example, the movement of ice floes in the Arctic Ocean, the changing size of the Antarctic Ice Shelf, and how icebergs form and break up would all fall under the study of glaciology.

This science does not focus only on ice on planet Earth, though. Glaciologists are also involved in the search for evidence of ice and water on the planet Mars and on Europa, a moon of Jupiter on which spacecraft have detected signs of ice. By looking at the landscape, they can detect signs of water and ice, such as landforms that appear to have once been riverbeds, or valleys and gorges that may have been formed by glacial movements.

With the rapid changes in Earth's environment and the increasing successes related to the discovery of other planets, moons, comets, and other celestial bodies, glaciology will undoubtedly be an important science for generations to come.

What is the main idea of this passage?

_____

_____

_____

_____

_____

EXAMPLE 2

Identify THREE details from the passage in Example 1.

_____

_____

_____

_____

_____

_____

_____

_____

_____

_____

_____

_____

_____

_____

_____

_____

_____

_____

_____

_____

EXAMPLE 3

Using your answers from Examples 1 and 2, write a brief summary of this passage, being sure to include the main idea and three important details.

_____

_____

_____

_____

_____

_____

_____

_____

_____

_____

_____

_____

_____

_____

_____

_____

_____

_____

Using Your Own Words

When writing a summary, you should always use your own words rather than directly copying lines from the text. Using your own words helps you to convey the meaning of the story more easily, as well as avoid plagiarism. When you present a summary in your own words, you explain what the story or article was about using your own terminology and language.

To help you use your own words when summarizing, think about how you would verbally explain the written piece to a friend. Rather than recite specific lines of text, you would probably identify the main idea in your own everyday language and specify the most important details in a way that does not seem forced. When you have finished writing your summary, review it to be sure you have used your own words. If it contains terms that you are not very familiar with, or that you would not use in your ordinary conversations with others, then you should revise it so that it sounds like something you would say. For example, read this passage, taken from the opening lines of the Declaration of Independence.

> *When in the course of human events, it becomes necessary for one people to dissolve the political bands which have connected them with another, and to assume among the powers of the earth, the separate and equal station to which the laws of nature and of nature's God entitle them, a decent respect to the opinions of mankind requires that they should declare the causes which impel them to the separation.*

This is a very wordy sentence, whose meaning can be difficult to grasp. Rewriting it in your own words can make it easier for a reader to understand.

> *Sometimes people have to break away from their political allies so that they can rise up to a position where they are equal with them. It would be disrespectful not to explain to those allies why you are doing this, though, so allow me to present our reasons for doing so.*

While this summary does use some of the same words as the original, it obviously is not a verbatim (word-for-word) copy. This summary is also easier for you as a reader to understand than a simple recopying of the original text. By using your own words, you can make material much more comprehensible, or easier to read.

The only time you should include a word-for word copy of a piece of text is when specifically quoting a line from a story or article. Even that should be done sparingly, and when doing so, be sure to use quotation marks and give credit the original author and work.

EXAMPLE 4

Below you will find the Preamble to the U.S. Constitution. Read the text, and then rewrite it, using your own words. You may want to discuss some of the more difficult words with your class and your teacher before constructing your response.

> We the People of the United States, in Order to form a more perfect Union, establish Justice, insure domestic Tranquillity, provide for the common defence, promote the general Welfare, and secure the Blessings of Liberty to ourselves and our Posterity, do ordain and establish this Constitution for the United States of America.

_____

_____

_____

_____

_____

_____

_____

_____

_____

_____

_____

_____

_____

_____

_____

_____

Understanding the Underlying Meaning

One of the most important aspects of summarizing someone else's writing is being sure that you mirror the underlying meaning of the work, rather than just covering the details. You should understand what it is that you are summarizing, so that your summary will make sense. If your reader is familiar with the work that you are summarizing, and your summary is not true to the meaning of the original, then your overall paper will seem weaker and the reader will lose faith in your authority as a writer. If your reader is not familiar with the work that you are summarizing, your summary should provide enough information that he or she will grasp the underlying meaning of the original work.

A summary should capture the meaning and relevant details of a written piece, and not just provide a list of surface details. For example, read this passage.

> ### The Bundle of Sticks
> #### by Aesop
>
> An old man lying on his deathbed summoned his sons to give them some parting advice. He pointed to a bundle of sticks tied together in one corner of the room, and told his oldest son to break it. The boy picked up the bundle and tried as hard as he could, but was unable to break it. Each of the other sons took a turn trying to break the bundle of sticks, but despite their efforts, none could perform the task requested by their father.
>
> "Now untie the sticks, and each of you take one," the father told them.
>
> They did as he said, and each boy was easily able to break his stick for the old man.
>
> "I hope you understand my meaning," the old man said, and then he died.

If you were simply to summarize the facts of this passage, you would write something like

> An old man who was dying told his sons to break a bundle of sticks. None of them could. Then they untied them and broke them individually, after which the old man died.

While these few sentences do indeed summarize the facts from the story, they do not capture the underlying meaning, which is that people are stronger when they work together. A better way to summarize this passage, then, would be to include the underlying meaning, like so:

> *An old man who was dying wanted to teach his sons a lesson, so he asked them to try to break a bundle of sticks. Individually, they were unable to break the bundle, but when each took a single stick, they broke them easily. The father wanted them to understand that they should work together to achieve goals rather than try to accomplish difficult tasks on their own.*

This summary captures both the main idea of the passage and the underlying meaning. Even without reading the original story, the reader should have a strong grasp of what it was about.

EXAMPLE 5

Read this paragraph.

> Here are some facts about the effects of smoking. When you smoke, you significantly increase your chances of developing lung disease, heart disease, emphysema, hardening of the arteries, and cancer, each of which generally involves a long, slow, painful death. More immediate effects include yellowing of your teeth, bad breath, deadening of your taste buds, and the offensive smoke odor absorbed into the clothing of smokers. Cigarettes are becoming increasingly expensive as well, with a single pack costing over five dollars in many places. A carton of cigarettes can sell for over sixty dollars.

What is the underlying meaning of this passage?

Ⓐ   People should smoke.

Ⓑ   There are consequences for those who smoke.

Ⓒ   You should not take up smoking.

Ⓓ   Emphysema is a very serious disease.

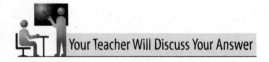 Your Teacher Will Discuss Your Answer

Read the following passage, and then complete the writing activity that follows.

On December 1, 1955, Rosa Parks was riding a bus in Montgomery, Alabama when she was told by the bus driver to give up her seat to a white man that had just boarded. The law at the time said that Ms. Parks had no claim to the seat, but she still refused to give it up. Because she refused to give up her seat, the bus driver stopped the bus, summoned a nearby police officer, and had her arrested.

At that time, there were a number of laws that were designed to deny African-Americans the rights enjoyed by white people. The law that said African-Americans had to give up their seats on the bus to any white person without a seat was unfair. She knew that obeying unfair laws would only lead to more mistreatment, and by refusing to give up her seat, she took a stand against anti-black rules.

Because she refused to give up her seat, she was arrested. By being arrested, she would be brought to court where her lawyers would have the chance to legally challenge the law requiring segregated buses. If she had not been arrested, then the attorneys would not have had a case to argue. If the case hadn't been argued, it never would have been challenged, and the Supreme Court never would have issued its ruling that overturned the bus law.

Finally, because she took a stand and was punished for it, other people became aware of the situation. Many were African-Americans who were inspired to organize a bus boycott, which struck back at the people who benefited from the unjust law. By taking a stand against the bus rule, Ms. Parks sparked a local revolution, which eventually grew throughout the country, and finally resulted in federal legislation that guaranteed racial equality. Without Rosa Parks, the country might still be segregated today.

Write a one-paragraph summary of this passage.

Be sure to

- include the main idea
- include significant details
- use your own words
- express the underlying meaning of the original passage

Go On

_____

_____

_____

_____

_____

_____

_____

_____

_____

_____

_____

_____

_____

_____

_____

_____

_____

_____

_____

_____

STOP

Writing Applications

Notes

Notes

Notes

Notes